P9-EDZ-252

1950

Volume VI # 1960

TIME LIFE BOOKS ®

This Fabulous Century

1950
1960

Volume VI

By the Editors of TIME-LIFE BOOKS

Time-Life Books, New York

TIME-LIFE BOOKS

FOUNDER: Henry R. Luce 1898-1967

Editor-in-Chief: Hedley Donovan
Chairman of the Board: Andrew Heiskell
President: James R. Shepley
Group Vice President: Rhett Austell

Vice Chairman: Roy E. Larsen

MANAGING EDITOR: Jerry Korn
Assistant Managing Editors: Ezra Bowen, David Maness,
Martin Mann, A. B. C. Whipple
Planning Director: Oliver E. Allen
Art Director: Sheldon Cotler
Chief of Research: Beatrice T. Dobie
Director of Photography: Melvin L. Scott
Senior Text Editor: Diana Hirsh
Assistant Art Director: Arnold C. Holeywell
Assistant Chief of Research: Myra Mangan

PUBLISHER: Joan D. Manley
General Manager: John D. McSweeney
Business Manager: Nicholas J. C. Ingleton
Sales Director: Carl G. Jaeger
Promotion Director: Paul R. Stewart
Public Relations Director: Nicholas Benton

THIS FABULOUS CENTURY

SERIES EDITOR: Ezra Bowen
Picture Editor: Mary Y. Steinbauer
Designer: Charles Mikolaycak
Assistant Designer: Jean Lindsay Morein
Text Associate: Carlotta Kerwin
Staff Writers: Betsy Frankel, Sam Halper, Anne Horan,
Lucille Schulberg, Gerald Simons, David Thomson,
Bryce S. Walker, Edmund White, Peter Yerkes
Researchers: Alice Baker, Jill Beasley, Evelyn Constable,
Terry Drucker, Marcia A. Gillespie, Helen Greenway,
David Harrison, Helen M. Hinkle, Carol Isenberg,
Nancy J. Jacobsen, Myra Mangan, Mary Kay Moran,
Patricia Smalley, Gabrielle Smith, Johanna Zacharias
Design Assistant: Anne B. Landry

EDITORIAL PRODUCTION
Production Editor: Douglas B. Graham
Assistant Production Editors: Gennaro C. Esposito,
Feliciano Madrid
Quality Director: Robert L. Young
Assistant Quality Director: James J. Cox
Copy Staff: Rosalind Stubenberg (chief),
Susan B. Galloway, Florence Keith, Pearl Sverdlin
Picture Department: Dolores A. Littles,
Elizabeth A. Dagenhardt
Traffic: Carmen McLellan

The following individuals and departments of Time Inc. gave
valuable aid in the preparation of this book: Editorial Pro-
duction, Norman Airey; Library, Benjamin Lightman; Picture
Collection, Doris O'Neil; Photographic Laboratory, George
Karas; TIME-LIFE News Service, Murray J. Gart; Correspon-
dents Jane Beatty (Philadelphia), Pam Burke (Los Angeles),
Juliane Greenwalt (Detroit), Joan Larkin (San Francisco),
Frank Leeming Jr. (St. Louis), Holland McCombs (Dallas),
Jane Rieker (Miami), Gayle Rosenberg (Los Angeles), Phyllis
Wise (Washington, D.C.).

Contents

America
1950-1960

Wednesday afternoon mambo class, Palladium Ballroom, New York, 1954.

Lunchtime at State Park Marina, Long Island, 1958.

Drive-in movie, Moab, Utah, 1954.

Senior citizens in St. Petersburg, Florida, 1959.

Little Leaguers, Manchester, New Hampshire, 1954.

16

Auto showroom, Levelland, Texas, 1957.

Baton-twirling contest at Soldier Field, Chicago, 1957.

Painting class in Attica, Kansas, 1955.

Office buildings, Park Avenue, New York, 1959.

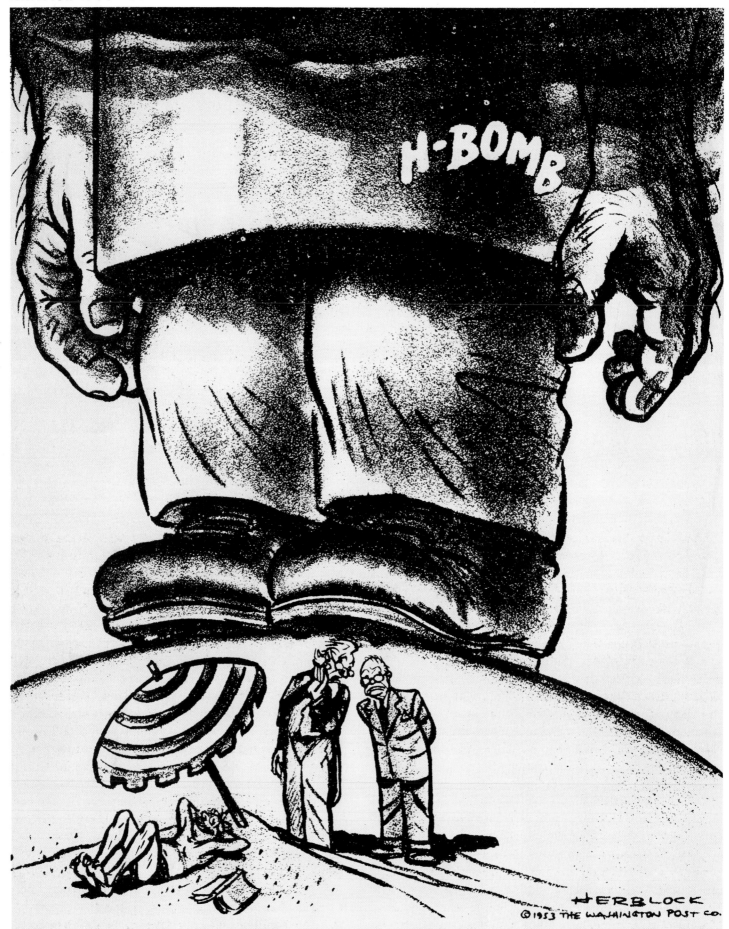

"THINK MAYBE WE'D BETTER SAY SOMETHING ABOUT IT?"

Three Minutes to Midnight

We have arrived at the point ... where there is just no real alternative to peace.

DWIGHT D. EISENHOWER

Shortly after the start of the New Year in 1951, with the sort of fanfare that only Hollywood could provide, Mrs. Ruth Colhoun, a Los Angeles mother of three, officially broke ground for her backyard atomic-bomb shelter. On hand were cheering starlets, studio flacks, TV cameras and representatives from the construction company that would dig the $1,995 underground cubicle at the edge of Mrs. Colhoun's patio and provide it with beige-painted concrete walls, green carpeting and storage space for canned food. The shelter was among the first of many *(pages 72-73)* that would be built throughout the nation during the new decade, and to Mrs. Colhoun it simply represented one of the sensible precautions of modern-day homemaking.

"It will make a wonderful place for the children to play in," she told reporters, "and it will be a good storehouse, too. I do a lot of canning and bottling in the summer, you know." But underneath Mrs. Colhoun's cheerful good sense there lurked an anxiety, a kind of prickling subcutaneous dread that no one in the '50s was fully able either to comprehend or to forget. Somehow, in a manner understood only by nuclear scientists, and for reasons clear only to a few senior statesmen, a bomb

might fall that could blow Los Angeles or the United States—or perhaps the globe itself—to smithereens.

Americans had been suffering from an increasingly severe case of jitters ever since the end of World War II. The victory that had thrust the United States into a position of world leadership had seemed at first a clear triumph of democracy and clean living; while the responsibilities were awesome, most Americans felt that the country deserved no less. But victory had quickly turned sour. The Soviet Union, with what seemed like sheer barbarian malice, had torn up its wartime agreement with the Allies and gobbled down half of Europe. Its armies stayed threateningly strong. By 1950 Russia had three times as many combat airplanes as the United States, four times as many troops, 30 tank divisions to America's one. Communism, obviously, was out to conquer the world. The only thing that prevented it was America's monopoly of the atomic bomb, that simple but terrifying solution to the problems of power politics: only five years before, the A-bomb had successfully obliterated Hiroshima, Nagasaki and 106,000 Japanese citizens, thus preventing combat casualties of an estimated one million clean-cut American GIs. Then, in the late summer of 1949, four months before the beginning of the new decade, the Soviet Union exploded its first atomic bomb.

The first inkling that Russia had the bomb came on a lazy August afternoon when an Air Force B-29 bomber returned from a routine scientific mission, measuring cosmic rays in the upper atmosphere. The plane carried photographic plates designed to record radioactive particles. Instead of showing the usual spattering of light tracks, the plates from this trip were saturated. The only explanation was an atomic blast. President Harry S. Truman was told the news in his oval office overlooking the White House rose garden. As he listened to the briefing, he shook his head and asked again and again, "Are you *sure?*" Then, finally convinced, he announced, "That means we have no time left."

But time for what? No one seemed to know how to react to the news. The State Department had developed no clear-cut contingency plans for the day that Russia would set off an A-bomb, and Defense had in fact begun further reducing the armed forces in an economy drive. What was more, most of the scientists who had worked on the Hiroshima bomb had left the atomic weapons laboratory at Los Alamos, New Mexico, to return to university campuses.

The Administration took three weeks making up its mind to tell the public what had happened. On September 23, while a sudden thunderstorm crashed over Washington pelting the White House roof with hail, Press Secretary Charles Ross closed the doors to the press room. With no conscious attempt at melodrama, he told correspondents, "Nobody is leaving here until everybody has this statement." He handed out a mimeographed release, and one reporter whistled. Then the doors were opened and the newsmen raced down the corridor to phone the story to their papers, breaking off the nose of a stuffed deer in their haste.

The public was stunned. All the horrors of Hiroshima seemed about to come home. Defense experts estimated that if the Russians ever decided to blast U.S. cities with A-bombs, 10 to 15 million people might die in a single day. "There is only one thing worse than one nation having the atomic bomb—that's two nations having it," Nobel Prize-winning chemist Harold C. Urey told reporters, and he echoed the fears of most plain citizens. The editors of the *Bulletin of the Atomic Scientists,* an influential professional journal, moved the hands of the clock that regularly appeared on its cover to an ominous three minutes before midnight.

Still, no one knew quite what to do. Behind tightly closed doors the Administration thrashed about for a solution. Its defense policy for the cold war had been to "contain" Communism behind its existing borders by beefing up threatened countries with billions of dollars in economic aid and staunch promises of military support. Just six months earlier, the U.S. had led in forming the North Atlantic Treaty Organization, a defense pact with Canada and 10 allies in Western Europe. But with America's monopoly of atomic weapons broken by its most dangerous enemy, none of these maneuvers seemed to offer real security.

One solution, almost as unpleasant to contemplate as the problem itself, nagged at the minds of the planners. While working on the original uranium bomb, physicists at Los Alamos had tinkered with the idea of designing a superbomb, an apocalyptic weapon that would deliver its kick by fusing together atoms of hydrogen, the element that fuels the sun. And whereas technical problems limited the explosive potential of the uranium-powered A-bomb, the hydrogen bomb could be made as powerful as any peace-loving nation could possibly want. It was possible, in theory, to build an H-bomb a thousand times more potent than the Hiroshima weapon or even one large enough to incinerate entire populations. In a decade that put so much stock in keeping up with the Joneses, here was an obvious way to stay ahead of the Russians.

Under the shadow of these awesome possibilities, the top echelons of government and science argued the feasibility—and morality—of building an H-bomb. Most of the scientists were opposed. Many felt a gnawing guilt that they had contributed to the slaughter of the Japanese cities. Few relished the prospect of working on an even more devastating weapon. J. Robert Oppenheimer, the soft-spoken, frail-looking genius who had headed the A-bomb project at Los Alamos, summed up their feelings: "In some crude sense, which no vulgarity, no humor, no overstatement can quite extinguish, the physicists have known sin and this is a knowledge which they cannot lose."

Furthermore, Oppenheimer believed the superbomb might prove impossible to build. "I am not sure the miserable thing will work, nor that it can be gotten to target except by ox-cart," he wrote. "That we become committed to it as a way to save the country and the peace appears to me full of dangers." And when Oppie spoke, others listened. A linguist, poet and a scholar of Sanskrit philosophy as well as the interiors of atoms, he was a kind of intellectual Galahad to other physicists *(pages 48-49)*. Two months after the detonation of Joe (for Stalin) One, as the Russian blast was dubbed, eight of the Atomic Energy Commission's nine-man panel of scientific advisors urged President Truman to shelve all plans for the super.

But in the end the building of the H-bomb was inevitable, partly because of the maverick persistence of a brilliant, Hungarian-born physicist named Edward Teller. Ever since 1945, Teller had been fascinated by the technical possibility of fusing the hydrogen atom. In some ways, Teller was the quiet-mannered Oppenheimer's diametric opposite. Stocky, beetle-browed, with tousled hair and rumpled suits, he exhibited an odd mixture of intellectual virtuosity and stubbornness that often grated on other scientists. In his student days in Munich, a streetcar had run over his right foot, which had to be amputated above the ankle; he wore a leather foot. Nevertheless, he doggedly tramped up mountains for exercise. With the same doggedness, he pestered the AEC, the military and Congress to let him try to build the hydrogen bomb.

Teller's voice was the one the Administration wanted to hear. Essentially the H-bomb was born of fear of Communism, fear of Russia's superior armies, fear perhaps of the responsibilities of world leadership, fear that the Russians—by hook or crook—might get the superbomb first. On January 27, 1950, one of these fears seemed partially confirmed when Dr. Klaus Fuchs, a British physicist who had worked on the A-bomb at Los Alamos, confessed that from 1942 to 1949 he had fed atomic secrets to the Soviet Union. The shock hit Washington with even greater force than the news of Joe One. "I don't think you have a choice," Rear Admiral Sidney W. Souers of the National Security Council told President Truman. "It's either we make it or wait until the Russians drop one on us without warning." Four days after Fuchs' revelation, Truman announced that work on the H-bomb would begin.

That summer, the nation's concern about Communist aggression was vindicated. On June 25, 1950, a massive invasion force from Communist North Korea rolled into South Korea, and within a month the Red troops had occupied most of the peninsula. Truman, backed by the U.N. Security Council, ordered American GIs to the battlefield, and on July 1 Major General William F. Dean landed in Pusan with an advance battalion of the 24th Infantry Division. For the second time in five years, the United States was at war.

With the issue joined, the nation shook off its bewilderment and began the familiar process of mobilization. Draft boards stepped up their calls of eligible young men, Congress voted immense new riches for the military, and industry tooled up to deliver jet planes and hand grenades. Though nobody expected the North Koreans to lob any A-bombs at American cities, civil defense organizations hustled to deal with the potential Russian threat. Air-raid drills became routine in public schools, and frightened first graders and blasé highschoolers marched into corridors and basements to crouch among the steam pipes until the all-clear.

Many citizens, like Mrs. Colhoun of Los Angeles, soon

Text continued on page 30.

THREE MEN IN A TUB

Battlefield reverses early in the Korean war indicated to at least one critic that politicians of both parties were uncomfortably at sea.

"LOOK OUT, HARRY, HERE COMES A LIBRARY"

Amid reports of federal scandals involving gifts from lobbyists, a new hullabaloo arose over solicitations for a Truman Library.

"I'M FINE. OF COURSE, EVERY ONCE IN A WHILE I GO LIKE THIS—"

Jittery stock prices in 1957 reflected the beginning of a nine-month economic slump after several years of unprecedented prosperity.

SHOOTIN' WORDS!

In 1958 and 1959 Alaska and Hawaii were voted in as the 49th and 50th states, the first to be added to the Union in 47 years.

"WHAT'S OUR FIRM, UNSWERVING ASIA
POLICY THIS WEEK?"

Pleas from the French in 1954 to aid them in their war in Indochina produced much rhetoric—and vacillation—from the Administration.

DOG DAZE

Russia's second satellite, launched November 3, 1957, carried a dog —while America's missile program was still solidly grounded.

INCH BY INCH

In 1960, six years after the Supreme Court had ordered public schools to integrate, 2,118 U.S. school districts still had not complied.

CLOAK-AND-DAGGER MAN

After a U-2 spy plane was shot down over the Soviet Union on May 1, 1960, the Russians angrily walked out of a summit meeting.

began building their own bomb shelters and stocking them with everything from Geiger counters and oxygen tanks to Virginia hams, volumes of Shakespeare and cases of Scotch. Corporations like DuPont and U.S. Steel authorized bombproof chambers for company records, and *Chicago Tribune* publisher Colonel Robert R. McCormick built a concrete cavern for himself and the staff. Mrs. Alf Heiberg, a onetime spouse of Douglas MacArthur, planned a grandiose shelter large enough to accommodate 100 friends. "After all," she told reporters, "if they attacked Washington I'm sure they'd aim a bomb at a former wife of General MacArthur."

In a hubbub of general misinformation, all kinds of amateur authorities began offering advice on what to do when the bomb dropped. One man advised shaving dogs and cats to prevent their fur from becoming radioactive. Another proposed a drawstring bag, to be yanked over the head in times of peril. Still others suggested aluminum pajamas, lead girdles and lead-foil brassieres. A patent-medicine mixer tried to market a "U-235 Atomic Shock Cure," but was stopped by the Public Health Service when it discovered the active ingredients—table salt, bicarbonate of soda and water.

Meanwhile, a team of scientists headed by Edward Teller quietly continued work on the super in the secrecy of Teller's laboratory at Livermore, California. At last, in the fall of 1952, they moved shiploads of ion chambers, high-speed cameras, beta-ray spectrographs, uranium and heavy hydrogen, and other nuclear paraphernalia to Eniwetok, an atoll in the Marshall Islands in the Pacific, and prepared to test the first H-bomb. On November 1, 1952, while scientists peered through special smoked glasses on ships and planes 50 miles away, the largest explosion ever created by man obliterated an entire island and confirmed that now man had a weapon for which there was no known defense.

The scientists themselves were awed by the power of the blast. The heat at its center was at least five times as great as that at the interior of the sun. It produced a cloud of radioactive coral dust and water that rose like a gigantic cauliflower, blue and gray-green and mauve, some 25 miles into the stratosphere, and spread a hundred miles across the sky. A year and a half later, when the figures were made public, the nation learned that if the device had been exploded over New York City its fireball would have extended almost four miles, vaporizing everything from Central Park to Washington Square. It would have gouged out such a crater that the Hudson and East Rivers would have flowed together across midtown, dividing Manhattan into two separate islands. The destruction of other cities was projected in alarming diagrams that showed sinister bull's-eyes superimposed over city maps. All of Washington, D.C., would have gone, all of San Francisco and Spokane, and most of St. Louis and Pittsburgh.

The AEC had imposed strict secrecy on the Eniwetok test, but nothing so mighty could be kept quiet. Sailors on ships surrounding the blast sent home letters that had an apocalyptic ring. "It would take at least ten suns" to equal the light of the explosion, one man wrote. Another reported in detail: "About 15 minutes after shot time, the island on which the bomb had been set off from, started to burn and it turned a brilliant red. It burned for about six hours. During this time it was gradually becoming smaller. Within six hours an island that had once had palm trees and coconuts had now nothing. A mile wide island had disappeared."

Back home, the doomsday predictions grew louder than ever. With the world's cities destroyed, civilization would end. Radiation might poison the atmosphere, killing off all life. The Teller bomb had the force of five megatons—five million tons—of TNT. Some people found megatons easy to translate into megadeaths. But most people wanted to forget about it.

The nation had suffered enough foreboding. Even in the shadow of the mushroom cloud, life trudged on. As the war in Korea tapered off to a stalemate, Americans began closing their bomb shelters and setting up barbecue pits. They cheered the 1952 election of Dwight Eisenhower, an old soldier who promised peace and who brought a material prosperity unequaled in memory. People settled down in front of their TV sets to watch *Gunsmoke,* in which violence struck at a slower and more understandable pace. They took dance lessons and went to college in unprecedented numbers, and they applauded the adventurous spirit of a New Zealander named Edmund Hillary who climbed to the top of Mt. Everest. They abandoned the bomb to the scientists and the cold war to the statesmen.

Yet under the surface the fears still simmered—the fear of Communism, the fear of subversion, the fear of war, the fear of annihilation. Every year or so an uncomfortable event would bring the anxieties into the open: a Russian H-bomb explosion in Siberia in 1953, just nine months after the U.S. test; a second American test at Bikini atoll in 1954 that accidentally—and for one man, fatally—showered a boatload of Japanese fishermen with radioactive coral dust; a scary new foreign policy announced by Secretary of State John Foster Dulles, who declared in 1956 that the U.S. would go to the brink of war to combat Communism; the unveiling in 1957 of a Russian intercontinental missile that could deliver instant holocaust almost anywhere on earth; and, five weeks later, the Soviet launching of a 184-pound bundle of radio transmitters called *Sputnik*—the Russian term for "traveling companion."

At the very end of the decade, even while President Eisenhower and Premier Khrushchev were meeting in a spirit of unexpected bonhomie at Camp David, Maryland, Americans were shivering at a movie called *On the Beach,* from the novel by Nevil Shute. The film depicted in lugubrious detail the end of life on earth in the aftermath of nuclear war. And in a recorded performance in Cambridge, Massachusetts, a graveyard humorist named Tom Lehrer evoked hollow chuckles in 1959 by putting into one gruesomely funny song the resignation the nation felt toward the bomb: "And we will all go together when we go,/Every Hottentot and every Eskimo;/When the air becomes uranious,/We will all go simultaneous,/Yes, we will all go together when we go."

DOOMSDAY CALENDAR

I have directed the Atomic Energy Commission to continue its work on all forms of atomic weapons, including the so-called hydrogen, or super bomb.
PRESIDENT HARRY S. TRUMAN, JANUARY 31, 1950

Radioactive poisoning of the atmosphere and hence annihilation of any life on earth has been brought within the range of technical possibilities. . . . In the end, there beckons more and more clearly general annihilation.
ALBERT EINSTEIN, FEBRUARY 12, 1950

North Korean forces invaded Republic of Korea territory at several places this morning.
CABLE FROM U.S. EMBASSY IN SEOUL, JUNE 25, 1950

The Soviet government deems it necessary to report that the United States has no monopoly in the production of the hydrogen bomb.
PREMIER GEORGI MALENKOV, AUGUST 8, 1953

Local defense must be reinforced by the further deterrent of massive retaliatory power.
SECRETARY OF STATE JOHN FOSTER DULLES, JANUARY 12, 1954

It is no longer a question of two nations, or groups of nations, devastating each other, but of all the future generations of all nations, who will forever pay, through disease, malformation, and mental disability, for our folly.
JOSEPH ROTBLAT, ENGLISH PHYSICIST, JUNE 1955

The ability to get to the verge without getting into the war is the necessary art. If you cannot master it, you inevitably get into war. If you try to run away from it, if you are scared to go to the brink, you are lost.
SECRETARY OF STATE JOHN FOSTER DULLES, JANUARY 1956

We will bury you! NIKITA KHRUSHCHEV, NOVEMBER 1956

The first artificial earth satellite in the world has now been created. This first satellite was successfully launched in the U.S.S.R.
TASS, THE SOVIET NEWS AGENCY, OCTOBER 5, 1957

If these provocations continue, we will have to aim our rockets at the bases.
NIKITA KHRUSHCHEV
ON AMERICA'S U-2 SPY-PLANE INCURSIONS, MAY 1960

Personalities

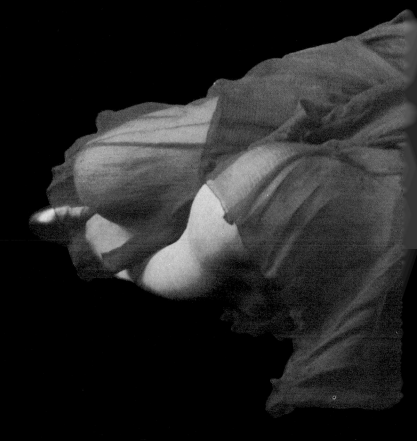

Sex queen Marilyn Monroe curls up languidly.

Living Symbols of an Era

I like Ike, too. ADLAI E. STEVENSON

In the fast-changing '50s, Americans quickly raised up new heroes and brought old ones crashing down. A Baptist minister, Martin Luther King, helped organize a bus boycott in Montgomery, Alabama, and emerged as spokesman of the burgeoning Negro civil rights movement. The young actor James Dean made a movie, *Rebel Without A Cause,* and became a symbol for his generation. Atomic scientist J. Robert Oppenheimer entered the decade a hero but within three years his character had been cast in doubt by witch-hunting bureaucrats.

Amid these vicissitudes of fame, the foremost personality of the decade maintained his phenomenal hold on the country's affections. He was Dwight D. Eisenhower, the vastly appealing man whose radiant grin was said to be "worth 10 divisions" in war and turned out to be worth a record 33 million votes in time of peace. As one Pennsylvania housewife said when Ike was elected President in 1952: "It's like America has come home."

Coming home to politics as a 61-year-old novice after 40 years in the Army, Ike nonplussed his rivals. Senator Taft, who lost the 1952 Republican Presidential nomination to the General, found Ike's politics so vague as to be unassailable; a frustrated Taft man said in despair, "It looks like he's pretty much for home, mother and heaven." And though the nation's leading Democrat, Adlai Stevenson, admitted *(above)* that he could not help being fond of Eisenhower, most liberals and intellectuals definitely did not like Ike. They attacked him for failing to announce support for the Supreme Court's "deliberate speed" decision on school integration and deplored his unabashed friendship with business tycoons: "All his golfing pals are rich men he has met since 1945," groused rich young Senator Jack Kennedy.

But Ike sailed serenely forward, obviously enjoying the role of a home-grown, open-minded moderate. Moreover, there was some evidence that his platitudes and circumlocutions derived less from fuzzy thinking than from political shrewdness. Once, when Ike's press secretary, Jim Hagerty, warned that reporters might ask a sensitive question, Ike reassured him. "If that question comes up," he said, "I'll just confuse them."

But to most people it did not matter that Ike appeared noncommittal; they felt they knew what he meant and liked him for it. And that was good enough for Ike, who declared he wanted nothing more than that Americans say, "He has been fair. He has been my friend."

On vacation from the White House, Ike goes fishing with his seven-year-old grandson David on the Fraser River in Fraser, Colorado.

Sad, bad James Dean smolders with the lonesome appeal that won him the ultimate teen-age accolade: "Everything he said was cool."

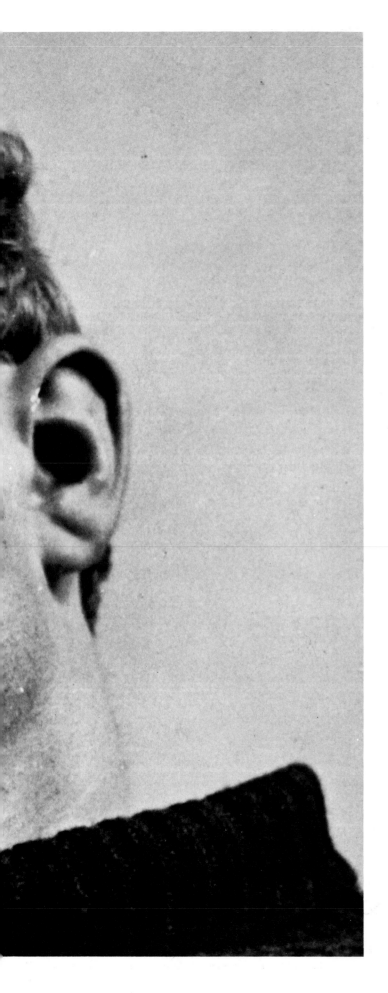

The Lost Boy

James Dean was every teen-age boy's inner vision of himself, and every girl's dream. His image was summed up by the title of his most famous movie, *Rebel Without A Cause*, in which he played the sensitive adolescent fighting a world of conformity. When he was killed in his car, at dusk on September 30, 1955, the kids made his ghost the focal point of their rebellion; their passion for him is analyzed below by novelist John Dos Passos.

There is nothing much deader
than a dead motion picture actor, and yet,
even after James Dean had been some years dead,
*   when they filed out of the close darkness*
and the breathedout air of the second and third
and fourth run motion picture theatres
where they'd been seeing James Dean's old films,
they still lined up:
*   the boys in the jackboots and the leather jackets,*
the boys in the skintight jeans, the boys in broad
motorbike belts, before the mirrors in the restroom
to look at themselves and see James Dean;
*   the resentful hair, the deep eyes*
floating in lonesomeness, the bitter beat look,
the scorn on the lip. . . .
*   The girls flocked out dizzy with wanting*
to run their fingers through his hair,
to feel that thwarted maleness; girl-boy almost,
but he needs a shave . . .
"Just him and me in the back seat of a car."
*   Their fathers snort, but sometimes they remember:*
"Nobody understood me either. I might have amounted
to something if the folks had understood."
The older women struggle from their seats weteyed.

The Embattled Hero

In June 1950 North Korean troops invaded South Korea, and the U.S.—and the U.N.—rallied to South Korea's defense. Americans nodded with confident approval as General Douglas MacArthur, the great hero of the Pacific in World War II and later supreme commander of the occupation troops in Japan, was appointed commander of the United Nations forces. Ten months later, Americans reacted with shock when MacArthur, having flouted U.S. policy by publicly advocating the bombing and blockading of Communist China, was summarily removed from his command by President Truman. Already frustrated and divided by the costly victory-less Korean "police action," the nation and its hard-pressed leaders lined up in two ranks, pro-MacArthur and anti-MacArthur.

The partisans were at full cry *(below)* when the General, calm and imperious, arrived home to find the people of the country in the throes of an emotional binge of which he was the focal point. Everywhere he went, vast crowds cheered him, and millions of people turned on their TV sets for his dramatic address to Congress. " 'Old soldiers never die,' " MacArthur intoned at the end, " 'they just fade away.' And like the old soldier of that ballad, I now close my military career and just fade away—an old soldier who tried to do his duty as God gave him the light to see that duty. Goodbye." It was good theater, and many people urged MacArthur to press ahead with a bid for the Presidency. But true to his word, he did fade—into the board of directors of Sperry-Rand—as a Senatorial hearing confirmed Truman's position that the General had ventured into the area of policy where only civilians should tread.

I believe we must try to limit the war to Korea for these vital reasons: to make sure that the precious lives of our fighting men are not wasted; to see that the security of our country and the free world is not needlessly jeopardized; and to prevent a third world war.

A number of events have made it evident that General MacArthur did not agree with that policy. I have therefore considered it essential to relieve General MacArthur so that there would be no doubt or confusion as to the real purpose and aim of our policy.

PRESIDENT HARRY S. TRUMAN

When you put on a uniform, there are certain inhibitions which you accept.

GENERAL DWIGHT D. EISENHOWER

In the opinion of the Joint Chiefs, [MacArthur's] strategy would involve us in the wrong war, at the wrong place, at the wrong time and with the wrong enemy.

GENERAL OMAR BRADLEY

His dismissal by the President is the culmination of disastrous failure of leadership in Washington.

GOVERNOR THOMAS E. DEWEY, NEW YORK

If MacArthur had his way, not one Asian would have believed the U.S. has a civilian government.

SOCIALIST NORMAN THOMAS

I do not think a general should make policies.

MRS. ELEANOR ROOSEVELT

Our only choice is to impeach President Truman.

SENATOR WILLIAM JENNER, INDIANA

We must never give up that the military is subject to and under control of the civilian administration.

SPEAKER OF THE HOUSE SAM RAYBURN, TEXAS

President Truman has given [the Communists] just what they were after—MacArthur's scalp.

SENATOR RICHARD M. NIXON, CALIFORNIA

A strong pillar in our Asian defense has been removed.

FORMER PRESIDENT HERBERT HOOVER

Snapping out orders during the brilliant Inchon landing, General Douglas MacArthur reaches his high point as Allied commander in Korea.

The Athlete Supreme

On May 25, 1951, the public address system at Philadelphia's Shibe Park boomed: "Now batting, Number Twenty-Four, centerfielder, Willie Mays." And lithe William Howard Mays, 20, stepped to the plate. No young ballplayer since Joe DiMaggio had arrived in the major leagues bearing more talent or promise. But as the crowd of 21,820 watched, poor Willie struck out. In his next 26 times up he managed one lone hit and fans began to write him off as one more wet skyrocket. Then suddenly, all that talent, all that promise came together in a beautiful rush *(below)*. Willie began to hit and run and throw with dazzling style. He became Rookie of the Year as the Giants won the pennant in 1951; Player of the Year as they swept the World Series in 1954; and by decade's end the only question left to be asked about Willie was this: Had anyone ever been better?

I saw a young kid of an outfielder I can't believe. He can run, hit to either field and has a real good arm. Don't ask any questions. You've got to get this boy.

NEW YORK GIANTS SCOUTING REPORT ON WILLIE MAYS, AGE 16

You can't make it better than he is. He does it every day that passes. There is no way you can pick it apart. He is the most valuable player in baseball and no one's close. He has the gifts and the temperament and the baseball records substantiate his claim with arithmetic. He is also a ballplayer to cherish because his exuberance is what you take away from a ball park and hold onto forever, to put with the small keepsakes of a lifetime. This is the player of the year. He might be the player of all the years since baseball has been played.

NEW YORK POST COLUMNIST JIMMY CANNON

Everything he does on a ballfield has a theatrical quality. . . . In the terms of my trade, Willie lifts the mortgage five minutes before the curtain falls. He rescues the heroine from the railroad tracks just as she's about to be sliced by the midnight express. He routs the villain when all seems lost. Willie has that indefinable thing called color. Color blended with talent brings the highest prices in the amusement market. Those blessed with both have what it takes at the box office.

ACTRESS AND BALL FAN TALLULAH BANKHEAD IN *LOOK*

Wheeling around second base on a long hit, Willie Mays glances at the outfield and heads toward third in a 1957 Giants-Braves game.

At his first press conference (above), Charles E. Wilson speaks slowly to make sure "You people aren't putting words into my mouth."

The Pentagon Businessman

As one of President Eisenhower's initial gestures of friendliness to American business, he appointed as his Secretary of Defense Charles E. Wilson, president of General Motors. Nicknamed "Engine Charlie," the new Secretary found himself in a political hot seat that required not only executive drive but restraint. Alas, restraint was not Engine Charlie's long suit. He soon embarrassed the Administration by asserting "what was good for our country was good for General Motors, and vice versa." This was quoted by the liberal press in the vice-versa form: "What's good for General Motors is good for the country." He later brushed off critics of a Pentagon expenditure by quipping, "I didn't come down here to run a grocery store."

Such straight-from-the-hip remarks kept coming as Wilson repeatedly spoke his mind (below). Administration critics declared that Wilson suffered from "hoof-in-mouth disease"; Engine Charlie contended, "You have to try to understand what a man means and not what he says." Despite the gaffes, Wilson did a creditable job running his enormous store ($40 billion per year, or 60 per cent of all federal expenses). And when he retired in 1957, the Eisenhower Cabinet lost an able administrator—and surely its most colorful one.

ON THE EXPLORATION OF SPACE: *I have enough problems here on earth.*

ON RED TAPE: *No inanimate thing will move from one place to another without a piece of paper that goes along telling someone where to move it.*

ON FOREIGN REACTION TO U.S. TROOPS ABROAD: *It is like having some of your relatives come to visit you. You are pleased to see them to begin with, but if they come to stay, you get tired of it.*

ON UNEMPLOYMENT AND WELFARE: *A man mustn't think he's sick because he sweats. . . . I've always liked bird dogs better than kennel-fed dogs myself—you know, one who'll get out and hunt for food rather than sit on his fanny and yell.*

ON HISTORY: *It's futile to talk too much about the past . . . like trying to make birth control retroactive.*

ON TRADE WITH IRON CURTAIN COUNTRIES: *I come from a long line of ancestors who believe you shouldn't sell firearms to the Indians.*

ON EXPERTS: *An expert is a mechanic away from home.*

ON GIVING ORDERS: *It's just like telling someone how to suck eggs. Let 'em suck at it in their own way.*

ON POLITICAL ETHICS: *There's an old political saying: "If your political opponent accuses you of being a liar, don't deny it. Accuse him of being a horse thief." I don't enthuse much over it.*

ON CHARLIE WILSON: *I am like the dog behind the Iron Curtain. It came across to West Germany one day and met another dog. They talked it over. Did he get enough to eat? Yes, he got enough to eat. Well, what was it he didn't like over there? He said: "Well, I would like to bark when I want to."*

The Quiz Fizz

Charles Van Doren seemed perfect for the part of U.S. folk hero of the '50s. He was handsome, slim and loose-limbed in the all-American way; he was an English instructor at Columbia University at a time when teaching was becoming fashionable; and although he belonged to an eminent literary family, he was not above using high-style braininess to fight for some of the new money floating around in a decade of affluence.

The arena for Van Doren's heroics was the richest of the TV quiz shows, *Twenty-One*, on which two contestants were matched against each other on a ladder of questions. If a player missed, he was out. But if he answered correctly and chose to keep going, the questions got trickier and the payoff astronomical.

Van Doren hung on through the toughest questions, knocked off all rivals and received an all-time record payoff of $129,000. En route he won the devotion of 25 million televiewers who suffered with him as he struggled to name the only three baseball players who had made more than 3,500 hits ("Ty Cobb, Cap Anson and

. . . Tris Speaker") and to pinpoint the operatic character who sings the aria "Sempre libera" in *La Traviata* ("She sings it right at the end of the party given by . . . What's her name! Soprano. Her name is . . . Violetta"). Teachers showered him with letters of thanks for proving that a hard-working pupil could master even the toughest questions; mothers instructed their daughters to marry a boy like him, not like Elvis Presley.

But at decade's end, the gold-plated world of quiz shows came crashing down. In August 1958 one of Van Doren's defeated rivals, Herbert Stempel, told the New York District Attorney's office that the show was a fake; *Twenty-One* contestants were primed with answers until their popularity began to wane. A check of other quiz programs opened an eel-bucket of fraud so tangled that a Congressional subcommittee haled witnesses down to Washington to testify. There, Van Doren put on his last performance. But this time very few Americans cared to suffer with him as he groped to explain *(below)* why a man would sell himself out.

I *would give almost anything I have to reverse the course of my life in the last three years. I cannot take back one word or action; the past does not change for anyone. But I have learned a lot in those three years. I've learned a lot about good and evil. They are not always what they appear to be. I was involved, deeply involved, in a deception. Before my first actual appearance on "Twenty-One," I was asked by Albert Freedman [producer of the show] to come to his apartment . . . . He asked me if, as a favor to him, I would agree to an arrangement whereby I would increase the entertainment value of the program. He told me that giving help to quiz contestants was merely a part of show business. This was not true but perhaps I wanted to believe* him. *I was sick at heart. Yet the fact is that I unfortunately agreed, after some time, to his proposal. As time went on, the show ballooned beyond my wildest expectations. I had supposed I would win a few thousand dollars and be known to a small television audience. But from an unknown college instructor I became a national celebrity. . . . To a certain extent, this went to my head. I was almost able to convince myself that it did not matter what I was doing because it was having such a good effect on the national attitude to teachers, education and the intellectual life. At the same time I was winning more money than I had ever had or even dreamed of having. I was able to convince myself that I could make up for it after it was over.*

CONGRESSIONAL SUBCOMMITTEE HEARING, NOVEMBER 2, 1959

MR. VAN DOREN

proof booth on the TV quiz show "Twenty-One," Charles Van Doren pretends to grope for an answer he was given earlier.

Everygirl

The girl that every girl wanted to be was a zestful red-headed model named Suzy Parker. Suzy was a nonstop talker whose favorite subjects were herself and her sister, mannequin Dorian Leigh. Her modeling score for the decade was over 60 magazine covers and thousands of advertisements that paid her $100,000 a year. Suzy's appeal went beyond mere beauty. She had a chameleon-like quality of looking just right in any clothes in any setting—slinky red sequins for a *Life* cover or a couple of pillows and not much else for a nylon ad. In whatever guise, she gave off an air of repressed excitement, as one fashion editor put it, "like a girl you catch a glimpse of between planes at Gander, Newfoundland, wearing a trench coat." Most of the time, Suzy seemed just as caught up by the excitement as everyone else, as these unabashed comments by Suzy on Suzy indicate.

ON HER VERY PROPER TEXAS BACKGROUND: *I come from an average Ku Klux Klan family. Actually, I was really adopted by my sister Dorian's weird parents. I'm really the lost daughter of the Dauphin. I have royal blood in my veins, and that's why I always wear Royal Blue....*

ON SUCH IMAGINATIVE STORIES: *I don't tell lies. I merely embellish stories . . . the truth is so dull.*

ON GOD'S GREAT WORKS: *I thank God for high cheekbones every time I look in the mirror in the morning.*

The Tormented Scientist

On June 29, 1954, after long hearings, the Atomic Energy Commission refused to renew the security clearance of physicist J. Robert Oppenheimer, who had been in charge of developing the A-bomb. The decision found Dr. Oppenheimer guilty not of disloyalty but only of vague and wholly legal proclivities—mainly having Communist friends and "lacking enthusiasm" for the H-bomb project. The Commission fired Oppenheimer as a consultant, to the outrage of concerned journalists and much of the scientific community *(below)*.

The great majority of this country's leading physicists harbored the most profound doubts about the wisdom of making a vast investment in the hydrogen project. These doubts were in part moral. And why should they not be, since physicists are also human beings? . . . But the point is that the physicists had a right to be wrong. . . . This right—the privilege of making an honest error of judgment without being labelled a traitor—is basic to free science and a free society.

JOSEPH AND STEWART ALSOP, *WASHINGTON POST*

As citizens and scientists, we are deeply disturbed. . . . Our concern is not so much with Dr. Oppenheimer as an individual, honored and respected as he is by us, as with the larger considerations of the apparent change in the government security policy. . . . If the consequences to the individual of an unpopular or unwise decision are the same as the consequences of a disloyal act, then the making of decisions or taking of responsibility for vital programs will be shunned, and two important ingredients of national strength—faith in the individual's honesty of judgment and willingness to back one's opinions with action—will become increasingly rare.

STATEMENT SIGNED BY 214 SCIENTISTS, 1954

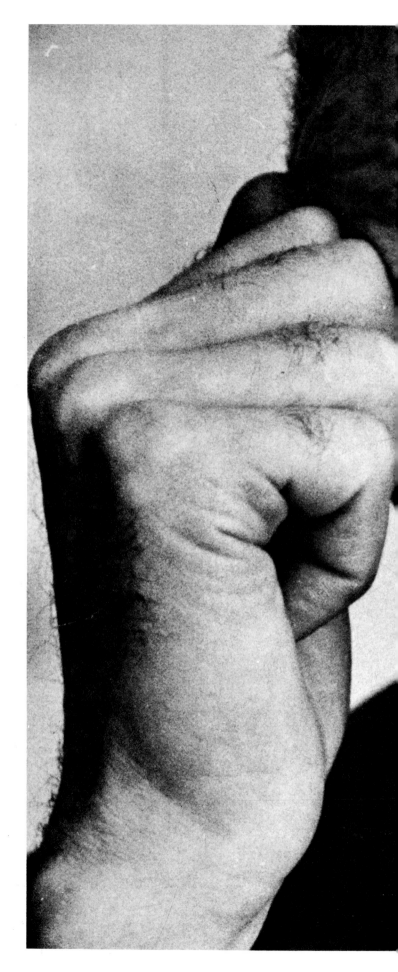

Atomic scientist J. Robert Oppenheimer, fired as a security risk, became a symbol of both repressed freedom and scientific morality.

The Egghead

At the Democratic Convention in 1952, Governor Adlai Stevenson of Illinois was a dark-horse candidate for the Presidency, strong in the party's ruling councils and in his own pivotal state of Illinois. As such, he was a natural choice to make the convention's welcoming address, which turned out to be a brilliant exercise both in political philosophy and phrase-making. America suddenly found herself with a candidate who was running on an intellectual ticket—and even winning many supporters from the G.O.P.'s homespun Dwight Eisenhower. One of Ike's backers described a typical supporter of the Governor as having "a large oval head, faceless, unemotional, but a little bit haughty and condescending." From this description came a graphic new synonym for any intellectual—"egghead." And Stevenson became the spiritual leader for all those who felt they fitted that mold. Throughout the 1952 campaign and for much of a reprise in 1956, his speeches *(excerpted below)* were high-minded and challenging, with a counterpoint of humor. But a war-weary country wanting respite and simple solutions twice rejected his candidacy overwhelmingly.

ON FREEDOM: *Tyranny is the normal pattern of government. It is only by intense thought, by great effort, by burning idealism and unlimited sacrifice that freedom has prevailed as a system of government. And the efforts which were first necessary to create it are fully as necessary to sustain it in our own day. He who offers this thing called freedom as the soft option is a deceiver or himself deceived. He who sells it cheap or offers it as the by-product of this or that economic system is knave or fool.*

ON EDUCATION: *The softness which has crept into our educational system is a reflection of something much broader, of a national complacency, of a confusion of priorities. . . . We have lacked, I fear, the deep inner conviction that education in its broadest sense unlocks the door of our future, and that it gives us the tools without which "the pursuit of happiness" becomes a hollow chasing after triviality, a mindless boredom relieved only by the stimulus of sensationalism or quenched with a tranquilizer pill.*

ON A CANDIDATE'S DAILY ORDEALS: *You must emerge, bright and bubbling with wisdom and well-being, every morning at 8 o'clock, just in time for a charming and profound breakfast talk, shake hands with hundreds, often thousands, of people, make several "newsworthy" speeches during the day, confer with political leaders along the way and with your staff all the time, ride through city after city on the back of an open car, smiling until your mouth is dehydrated by the wind, waving until the blood runs out of your arm, and then bounce gaily, confidently, masterfully, into great howling halls, shaved and all made up for television.*

ON HIS FUTURE AFTER DEFEAT IN 1952: *There are those who feel that I should devote my talents to the welfare of mankind by frequent talking. There is another smaller group who insist that God, and/or the electorate, has appointed me the scourge of the Republican Party. And finally there is a much smaller group that feels it is not unworthy or improper to earn a living. My sons are numbered in the latter group.*

Governor Adlai E. Stevenson gathers his thoughts—and his strength—during a peaceful visit to his family farm in Libertyville, Illinois.

51

The Apostle of Nonviolence

In Montgomery, Alabama, on December 1, 1955, an act of quiet courage reshaped the career of Martin Luther King Jr., a scholarly young preacher recently installed in his first church. That day a weary Negro seamstress defied the local law and refused to give up her bus seat to a white man. The woman's arrest was the last straw for Montgomery's Negro community; their leaders, including Dr. King, met to organize a one-day bus boycott.

On December 5, fully 90 per cent of the Negro populace walked or hitchhiked, but white authorities refused to budge and the Negroes' mild demands escalated into an all-out campaign for desegregated public transportation. King and his co-organizers set up a 200-car motor pool and underwrote the cost of their jitneys by raising about $225,000 in donations. And the Negroes honored King's pleas for nonviolence (*excerpted below*), despite arrests and harassments, capped by the bombing of King's home on January 30, 1956.

The boycott was almost a year old when, on November 13, 1956, the Supreme Court declared bus segregation illegal in Alabama. But despite this step on the road to equality, King's followers remembered his call for even greater effort: "If I am stopped, this movement will not stop, because God is with the movement."

ON PROTEST: *Nonviolence is the most potent technique for oppressed people. Unearned suffering is redemptive.*

ON VOTING RIGHTS: *All types of conniving methods are still being used to prevent Negroes from becoming registered voters. The denial of this right is a betrayal of the highest mandates of our democratic traditions. So our most urgent request to the President of the United States and every member of Congress is to give us the right to vote. Give us the ballot and we will no longer have to worry the federal government about our basic rights. Give us the ballot and we will no longer plead for passage of an anti-lynching law. Give us the ballot and we will transform the salient misdeeds of bloodthirsty mobs into the calculated good deeds of orderly citizens. Give us the ballot and we will fill the legislative halls with men of good will. Give us the ballot and we will place judges on the benches of the south who will do justly and love mercy and we will place at the head of the southern states governors who have felt not only the tang of the human but also the glow of the divine.*

ON INTEGRATION: *If we are arrested every day, if we are exploited every day, if we are trampled over every day, don't ever let anyone pull you so low as to hate. There is an element of God in every man.*

ON SEGREGATION: *Many [uneducated Negroes] unconsciously wondered whether they deserved better conditions. Their minds were so conditioned to segregation that they submissively adjusted to things as they were. This is the ultimate tragedy of segregation. It not only harms one physically but injures one spiritually.*

ON CIVIL DISOBEDIENCE: *I was proud of my crime. It was the crime of joining my people in a nonviolent protest against injustice. It was the crime of seeking to instill within my people a sense of dignity and self-respect. It was the crime of desiring for my people the unalienable rights of life, liberty, and the pursuit of happiness. It was above all the crime of seeking to convince my people that noncooperation with evil is just as much a moral duty as cooperation with good.*

Dr. Martin Luther King preaches his gospel of equality and nonviolence, giving the civil rights movement a new, nationwide impetus.

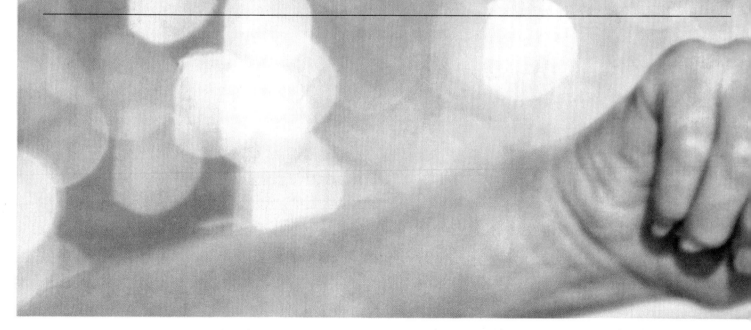

The Sex Symbol

Movie star Marilyn Monroe was a superblonde (37-23-37), the "sex symbol" of the decade. She received 5,000 fan letters a week and when she visited Japan, people fell into fish ponds to get a glimpse of the *shiri-furi* (buttock-swinging) actress. On screen Marilyn was a fluff-headed chippie; off screen she was a complex, unhappy person *(below)* obsessed with becoming a serious actress. In 1955 she told an interviewer in her baby voice that she would like to do Dostoevski. "Do you want to play *The Brothers Karamazov?*" the reporter asked. Her reply: "I don't want to play the brothers. I want to play Grushenka. She's a girl."

When you're famous you kind of run into human nature in a raw kind of way. It stirs up envy, fame does. People you run into feel that, well, who is she —who does she think she is, Marilyn Monroe? They feel fame gives them some kind of privilege to walk up to you and say anything to you, you know, and it won't hurt your feelings—like it's happening to your clothing. But one thing about fame is the bigger the people are or the simpler the people are, the more they are not awed by you! They don't feel they have to be offensive, they don't feel they have to insult you. You can meet Carl Sandburg and he is so pleased to meet you. He wants to know about you and you want to know about him. Or else you can meet working people who want to know what is it like. You try to explain to them. I don't like to disillusion them and tell them it's sometimes nearly impossible. They kind of look toward you for something that's away from their everyday life. I guess you call that entertainment, a world to escape into, a fantasy. Sometimes it makes you a little bit sad because you'd like to meet somebody kind of on face value. It's nice to be included in people's fantasies but you also like to be accepted for your own sake.

Biting playfully on a rhinestone earring, actress Marilyn Monroe silently sends across her personal message of pure sex appeal.

Fads

Viewers gawk through Polaroid glasses at a 3-D movie.

Davy, Deepies and Ducktails

The next person who mentions Davy Crockett to me gets a Davy Crockett flintlock over his head.

A DEPARTMENT STORE BUYER

Against a grim backdrop of the cold war and the space race, dozens of dizzy fads bubbled up in the '50s. A few of these, such as the building of bomb shelters and the sighting of mysterious flying saucers *(pages 68-69)*, were generated by the world news itself. Others, like ducktail haircuts and the college-bred nonsense of jamming dozens of people into a phone booth, were simply products of youth.

Some fads, however, were a product, period. In 1952 the movie industry, its audience cut in half by TV competition, was groping for a gimmick to get people back into the theaters when the Natural Vision Corporation came up with a hot idea called 3-D, or deepies. These were movies that gave a three-dimensional effect by simultaneously projecting two overlapping images, viewed by the audience through Polaroid glasses that refocused the two impressions into a single object.

The first full-length deepie, *Bwana Devil,* which premiered in Los Angeles on November 26, 1952, broke box-office records in its first week by grossing $95,000. Critics agreed that the script was awful (man-eating lions harass railroad builders in Africa), but the public loved the optical illusion of beasts that seemed to leap right out of the screen. To film makers who had doubted that people would go to movies where they had to wear special glasses, Bill Thomas of Paramount replied, "They'll wear toilet seats around their necks if you give 'em what they want to see!" But Thomas' optimism proved short-lived. The fad soon collapsed from the weight of its own dreary plots and by year's end the film trade conceded that 3-D stood for dead, dead, dead.

Meanwhile TV was generating some fads of its own, the most memorable being the cult of Davy Crockett. This one started on December 15, 1954, when an audience of 40 million (mostly between the ages of five and 15) watched lanky Fess Parker portray Davy on Walt Disney's weekly show *Disneyland.* Parker's folksy performance created a $100 million market for coonskin caps, Davy Crockett bathing suits, school lunch boxes and guitars. A record entitled "The Ballad of Davy Crockett" sold four million copies; and a merchant, stuck with 200,000 pup tents, stenciled Davy Crockett on them and sold them all in two days. But by July 1955, Davy's bull market turned b'arish; Crockett items began to pile up in stores, to the dismay of salesmen, one of whom lamented, "Kids are more fickle than women."

A four-year-old Davy Crockett checks out his coonskin cap. During the Crockett boom the price of coonskins soared to $8.00 a pound.

Cram Courses

*An outlandish spring rite called cramming—or, less
elegantly, stuffing—swept college campuses in the late '50s. The idea of the game
was to scrunch as many people or objects as possible into some small
space. It could even be done underwater—each of seven men from Fresno State held
his breath long enough to jam into a booth sunk in a swimming pool.*

Twenty-two California collegians pack into an outdoor phone booth.

Two Caltech boys adjust to a room stuffed with newspapers.

Forty students bulge out of a VW.

A Dizzying Success

In 1958 two California toy makers
heard about gym classes in Australia where kids
exercised with bamboo hoops and loved it.
Seizing upon the idea, their company, Wham-O,
began selling $1.98 plastic rings
called Hula-Hoops. Within six months American
kids were spinning 30 million
hoops put out by Wham-O and 40 imitators.

Kids compete in a Hula-Hoop derby at New Jersey's Brookside Swim Club. A 10-year-old boy set the club record at 3,000 spins.

Fads

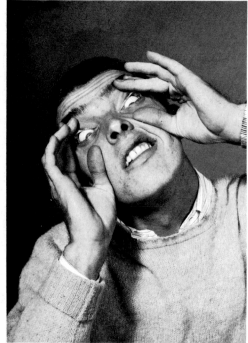

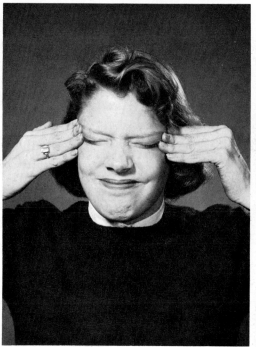

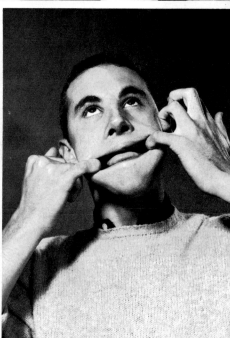

"DARN THESE CONTACT LENSES!"   "MOMMY, YOU MADE THE BRAIDS TOO TIGHT!"   "HELP! MY LOLLIPOP'S STUCK."

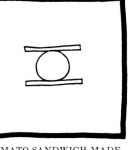

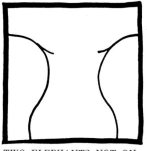

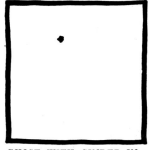

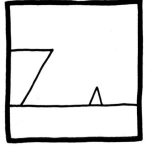

TOMATO SANDWICH MADE BY AMATEUR TOMATO SANDWICH MAKER

TWO ELEPHANTS NOT ON SPEAKING TERMS

GHOST WITH CINDER IN HIS EYE

SHIP ARRIVING TOO LATE TO SAVE DROWNING WITCH

GRANT'S TOMB AS SEEN BY ENGLISH SHEEP DOG

Droodles for Boodle

*One night in 1953, gag writer Roger Price persuaded TV emcee
Garry Moore to show his audience a batch of contrived
sketches he called Droodles. During the next week Price received
15,000 fan letters, and by the end of 1955, Price had published three
books of Droodles and had his own TV panel show. High
school kids carried the fad a step farther by inventing Living Droodles,
which required only a rubber face and a good punch line.*

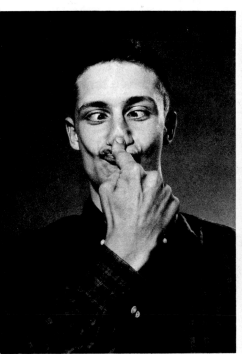

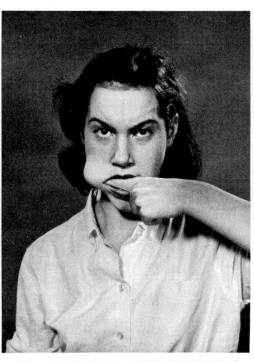

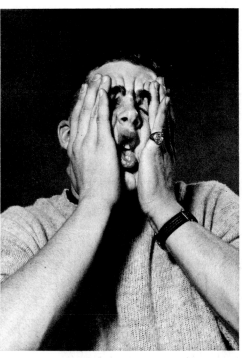

"JOHNNY! COME GET YOUR DART!"

"MADAM, PLEASE REMOVE YOUR UMBRELLA."

"MR. BUS DRIVER, MAY I COME IN?"

The Long Green

In 1952 the U.S. consumer market saw green. The tint came
from chlorophyll, a component of plants introduced into more than 90 products
that promised to make their users smell daisy fresh. Americans bought
the sweet promise, to the tune of some $135 million, until "The Journal of the
American Medical Association" pointed out that grazing
goats virtually live on chlorophyll and smell bad just the same.

New green toothpaste with miracle chlorophyll
NATURE'S GREATEST PURIFIER

GIVES YOU A

Clean Fresh Mouth All Day Long!

NOW—a new miracle toothpaste! It contains chlorophyll*, nature's greatest purifier. It destroys mouth odor instantly—and not for just minutes, but all day long. It fights *tooth decay* and *common gum troubles.*

This new green toothpaste is called Chlorodent. It was used in hundreds of tests by a leading independent research organization. The tests were made on men and women afflicted with bad breath. When they brushed their teeth with Chlorodent—

—*their mouth odor disappeared instantly!*
—*two hours later, their breath was still clean and fresh in 98% of the cases!*
—*four hours later* (at the end of the tests), *74% were still free of mouth odor!*

Chlorodent doesn't just cover up mouth odor, but *destroys* it. By using Chlorodent regularly—preferably after meals—you can be free of mouth odor all day long!

Chlorodent was perfected after four years of dental research. Try it. See why Chlorodent is winning friends *faster than any other toothpaste in America!*   *Water-soluble chlorophyllins

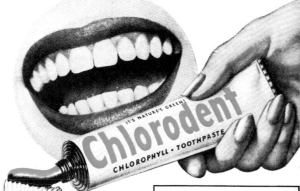

IT'S NATURE'S GREEN
Chlorodent
CHLOROPHYLL · TOOTHPASTE

THAT COOL, FRESH GREEN comes from nature's *chlorophyll*— the greatest deodorizing substance ever discovered!

What a difference Chlorodent makes!

"*I tried Chlorodent and now I wouldn't use anything else. I never dreamed my mouth could* [fee]*l fresh all day long.*"
Miss Pa[t]
Win[

Mouth odor is measured by scientific [o]smometer. It proved that Chloro[d]ent stops mouth odor far longer [t]han ordinary toothpaste.

Gum troubles cause half of all tooth losses, it has been estimated. Chlorodent promotes the growth of firm, healthy-pink tissue!

Tooth decay has been traced to mouth acids caused by bacteria. Chlorodent helps combat the bacteria . . . and reduces the acids!

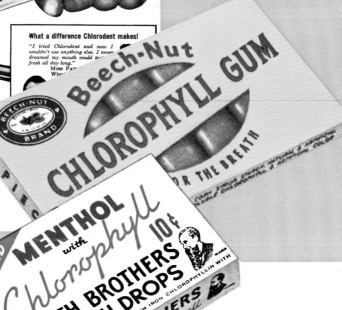

Pard
SWIFT'S DOG FOOD

CHLOROPHYLLIN ADDED

man's best friend

Beech-Nut BRAND
CHLOROPHYLL GUM
12 PIECES
[F]OR THE BREATH

New MEDICATED MENTHOL *with* **Chlorophyll** 10¢
SMITH BROTHERS COUGH DROPS
ACTIVE INGREDIENTS MENTHOL, POTASSIUM IRON CHLOROPHYLLIN WITH
SMITH BROTHERS
MENTHOL *with* *Chlorophyll*

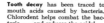

A New Pie in the Sky?

In 1947 a pilot flying near Yakima, Washington, spotted nine
"saucerlike things" moving at an estimated speed of 1,200 mph. His story caught
the imagination of the nation, kicking off the most bizarre fad
of the postwar years. By 1950 sightings of similar strange craft were being
made by excitable citizens all over the country and an average of 600
a year were reported during the decade. Meanwhile a harassed U.S. Air Force
spent some $60,000 annually to determine whether or not the whole
thing was just a big piece of pie in the sky. By decade's end no one knew.

Sheriff Wier Clem and his deputy search the sky of Levelland, Texas, for a flying saucer that was reported a few nights before.

A college student shows a drawing of a saucer he sighted. Behind him is another eerie craft "photographed" in New Mexico.

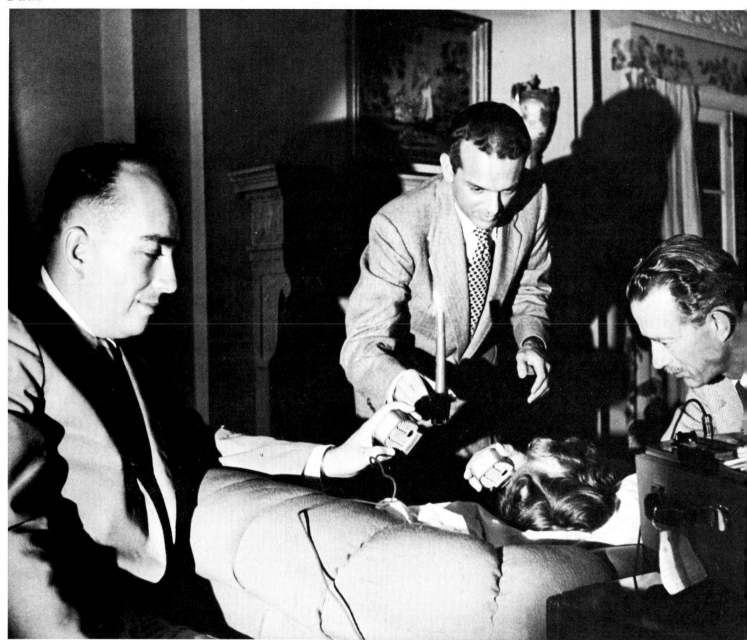

Hypnotist Morey Bernstein, discoverer of Bridey Murphy, holds a candle over subject Ruth Simmons in a reenactment of her trance.

The Ballad of Bridey

*In 1952 an amateur hypnotist, Morey Bernstein, put a Colorado
housewife known as Ruth Simmons into a trance—whereupon she began to dance an Irish jig
and announced in a rich brogue that she was one Bridey Murphy of 19th Century Cork
and Belfast. Bernstein subsequently wrote a bestseller about Bridey Murphy and thereby launched a
major fad. The spirit of Bridey invaded nightclub acts and private parties (right).
And in Oklahoma a 19-year-old boy committed suicide, explaining, "I am curious about the
Bridey Murphy story so I am going to investigate the theory in person."*

A composer (with folded hands) leads a supine songstress in a Bridey Murphy ballad.

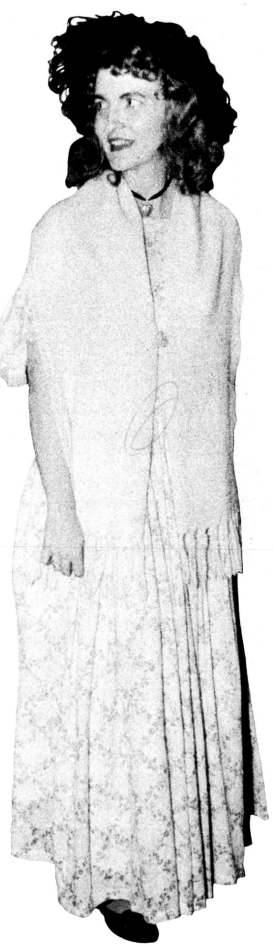

A come-as-you-were partygoer appears as Bridey.

THE Search FOR Bridey Murphy

BY MOREY BERNSTEIN

Bernstein's book sold over 170,000 copies.

A flame tops off the Reincarnation Cocktail.

The Big Boom's Reverberations

*Americans reacted to the reality of atomic power in widely differing ways.
The adventurous bought prospectors' kits and rushed off to the Colorado Plateau or the wilds of
Canada hoping for a strike of uranium. The timorous dug bomb shelters or bought prefab
ones, against the expected nuclear attack from Russia. Neither group made out very well. Few U.S.
ore-seekers made individual finds worth $100,000 or more. And shelter-owners
found little use for their expensive caves beyond storage of garden tools and old snow tires.*

Basic equipment for uranium prospectors included a $98.50 Geiger counter, sample ore, blank claim notices and a snakebite kit.

Equipment and Supplies Inventory

THREE-WAY PORTABLE RADIO	MATTRESSES AND BLANKETS (5)
AIR BLOWER by generator or by hand	AIR PUMP for blowing up mattresses
RADIATION DETECTOR	INCANDESCENT BULBS (2) 40 watts
PROTECTIVE APPAREL SUIT	FUSES (2) 5 amperes
FACE RESPIRATOR	CLOCK nonelectric
RADIATION CHARTS (4)	FIRST AID KIT
PICK AND SHOVEL COMBINATION for digging out after blast	FLASHLIGHT
GASOLINE DRIVEN GENERATOR	WATERLESS HAND CLEANER
GASOLINE 10 gallons	STERNO STOVE
CHEMICAL TOILET	CANNED WATER 10 gallons
TOILET CHEMICAL 2 gallons	CANNED FOOD meat, powdered milk, cereal, sugar etc.
BUNKS (5)	PAPER PRODUCTS

Above is a list of articles found in the $3,000 Mark I Kidde Kokoon. This shelter came with everything a family of five might need for a three- to five-day underground stay.

Some people bought commercial shelters; others designed their own.

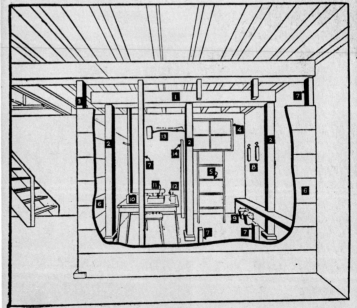

City's Proposal for Air Raid Shelter in Private Homes

The air raid shelter recommended for cellars of one and two-family dwellings by the Bomb Shelter Committee of the New York City Civil Defense Organization.

Key to above diagram:

(1) 6"x6" or larger girder placed under present floor beams to reduce span.

(2) 6"x6" wood posts or 4" diameter pipe columns, under girder about four feet apart.

(3) 6"x6" wood post or 4" diameter pipe column under present girder.

(4) Window for a second exit to outside. Should be covered on inside with heavy one-half inch mesh screening. A sandbag or heavy timber enclosure in the form of a well to the top of the window, should be placed outside of the window. The window should be fastened open at the air raid warning signal. The window should be at least 24"x24" in size.

(5) Ladder to window.

(6) Wood concrete or sandbag enclosure at least six feet high.

(7) 2"x4" wood studs, 24" apart for wood enclosure.

(8) Fire extinguishers.

(9) Pails of water.

(10) Battery operated radio.

(11) First-aid kit.

(12) Battery lantern.

(13) Axe.

(14) Crowbar.

The Bomb Shelter Committee said the shelter should be approximately eight feet by ten feet in size. The Committee said that an empty, concrete enclosed coal bin may be used as a shelter with the safety measures shown in the diagram.

Dressing Up and Down

*Fads in women's fashion ranged
from the hooded dress made of a single tube
shaped length of hip-clinging knit to the
skirt so full it required a crinoline underneath.
Dresses hung at mid-calf, but
shorts got shorter—with rolled-up cuffs.
Teenagers glittered with paste-on
rhinestones (below); while a favorite for working
girls was the pop-it necklace that could
be lengthened from choker to waist-length by
snapping on an extra string of beads.*

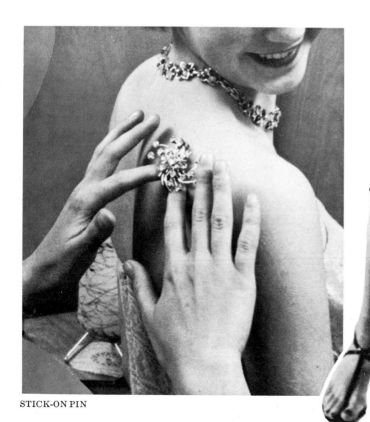

STICK-ON PIN

TUBE DRESS

SACK DRESS

POP-IT BEADS

SHORT
SHORTS

CRINOLINE

The swept-back ducktail

Poodles and Apaches

One of the most personal fads of the
'50s was the odd hairdo. Girls appeared in the
skull-hugging poodle and the pretty ones
got away with it. But boys who went for the swooping
ducktail or the starkly furrowed Apache
could find themselves in trouble:
in February 1957 a Massachusetts school
banned anyone with a ducktail.

The close-shaved Apache

Actresses (left to right) Denise Darcel, Peggy Ann Garner, Ann Sothern and Faye Emerson show off their curly poodle cuts in 1951.

Think Pink

The big fashion shocker of the '50s
was the emergence of pink from the underworld
of ladies' girdles into the charcoal
gloom of men's wear. In 1955 thousands of
pink shirts suddenly appeared
and pink soon spread to ties and even hatbands.
Other aberrations from the gray
flannel norm included Bermuda shorts in
offices and stringy Colonel ties and
pleated rogue pants in high-school classrooms.

Executives in Bermudas

Tiny polka dots brighten the old Colonel tie.

Baggy pegged pants appear at dance halls.

Surrounded by a variety of roseate haberdashery, a young man whips on a pink bow tie.

Rogue trousers feature a white side stripe.

Real George Is With It All the Way

Of all the fads that came and went in the '50s, perhaps the oddest was the disorientation of the English language. Styles in slang changed faster than the hemlines of Dior dresses, and words sometimes performed complete 180-degree turns in the course of the decade. Thus, "hot" in 1950 soon changed to "cool," "real gone" became "the most," what was "in" became "out," and soon "way, way out" was just about as "in" as one could get.

Adding to the confusion was the fact that different groups of people spoke their own particular slang. Jazz musicians conversed in one lingo, teenagers in another, hot rodders and space scientists in still others *(below)*, and Madison Avenue executives in something else again. But all groups shared one thing in common; nobody wanted to be labeled square *(opposite)*. For in a decade when everybody tried just as hard as possible to behave just like everyone else in his own circle (which meant, according to his friends, that he was either cool, hip, smooth, shoe, real George, tweedy, with it, tough or wild), the last place anyone wanted to be was out of it.

JAZZ AND BEBOP SLANG

CRAZY (*also "frantic," "the most"*) —wonderful, great; also a general response to anything anyone said, so that "What's new, Jack" would be answered by "Hey, crazy man."

DIG—to understand, appreciate, or even notice, as in "Dig that crazy mixed-up blonde."

CAT (*also "stud"*)—a person who dug; any man.

DOG—a song that did not make it.

GONE (*also "cool," "groovy," "far out," "the end"*)—the superlative of crazy.

FLIP—to become enthusiastic, as in "The cat really flipped over the chick."

HIP—aware; a cat who dug was hip.

HIPPY—any person who was so super-cool and far out that he appeared to be asleep when he was digging something the most.

BREAD (*also "geets," "green," "M"*) —money.

MEAN (*also "tough," "terrible"*)—words that replaced "crazy" to signify the greatest.

AXE—any musical instrument, from a saxophone to a piano.

BLOW—to play an axe, as in "He blows mean piano."

CHICK (*sometimes "sis"*)—a girl. An unattractive chick was a "bear" and a fat chick was known as "heavy cream."

MONKEY—a music critic. (He sees no music, hears no music, digs no music.)

TEEN-AGE LINGO

COOL (*also "neat," "smooth," "casual"*) —worthy of approval; as a noun, it denoted poise or self-assurance.

HANG LOOSE (*also "negative perspiration"*)—no sweat, don't worry.

HAIRY—formidable, as in a hairy exam.

CLUTCH—to panic, or lose one's cool.

YO-YO (*also "square," "nerd," "turkey," "spastic," "blow-lunch," "nosebleed"*)—a dull person; an outsider.

BLAST-OFF—go away, get lost, drop dead (*also "DDT" for "drop dead twice"*).

DRAG—anything, or anybody, that was considered dreary.

WHEELS—a car.

PASSION PIT—a drive-in movie.

GROUNDED—unable to borrow the family wheels to take a hot date to the passion pit.

SARC—sarcastic; a sarc remark would be, "Wanna lose ten ugly pounds? Cut off your head."

HARDEEHARHAR—the sarc response to someone else's bad joke.

HOT ROD ARGOT

DRAG—a race from a standing start.

BOMB (*also "screamer," "stormer," "hack," "draggin' wagon"*) —a souped-up car, or hot rod.

RAKING (*also "dagoing"*)—lowering the front end of a car to give it a streamlined look.

CHOPPING—lowering the roof of a car to give it a chopped top.

SKINS—tires; if they were whitewalls, they were called "snowballs."

DUALS (*also "stacks," "pipes," "Hollywoods"*)—a special exhaust system.

NERF-BAR—the bumper.

SPOOKING—a sophisticated term for bombing around, or driving someplace simply for the sake of driving.

SPACE SCIENCE GOBBLEDEGOOK

BIRD—a rocket, missile, earth satellite or any other inanimate flying object.

BEAST—a large bird.

IVORY TOWER—a vertical test stand.

STOVEPIPE—a missile's outside shell.

ELEPHANT EAR—a thick plate that reinforced hatches on the stovepipe.

SNAKEBITE—an accident.

EGADS BUTTON—pushed to blow up a missile that strayed off course, and thus might cause snakebite.

SQUARES ARE OUT

There are a hundred different uses of the word square. . . . Prowling into the subject in search of examples recently, the novelist Robert Sylvester heard these definitions from Manhattan to Montauk: "A square is someone who smokes without taking the band off his cigar; has luminous signs on his car bumpers . . . wears a pocket handkerchief with his initials showing . . . pays strict attention to all non-tipping signs; carries a portable radio to the ball game so he can follow the scores elsewhere; has trouble working the slots in the Automat; bothers to read the inscriptions on the photos of celebrities in restaurants; puts vermouth in a martini; and wears his hat brim a little wider than ours."

. . . Along Broadway, where the language acquires refinements—something like piling strawberries on the cheesecake at Lindy's—the squarest kind of square is called a cube. A cube is so square, they say, he can block his own hat. Another phrase for a real square is "way in," the opposite of someone real hip or "far out." Youngsters say: "He's a - - -," and finish the sentence by placing the index fingers together and drawing a square in the air. Another, somewhat sneakier way of calling someone a square in his presence is to describe him as an "L 7." By putting the letter and number like this—L 7—a crude square is formed.

Only the other day (jazz guitarist) Eddie Condon, asked about squares today, replied: "I don't use the word myself and never hear musicians who are professionals use it. I'd say that musicians who call people squares are squares." That squares the circle.

HERBERT MITGANG IN *THE NEW YORK TIMES MAGAZINE*

FINALIZE IS IN

My Madison Avenue etymologist, who has been assigned the task of keeping abreast of the English language employed by the ad people, blew in the other day, his brief case bulging. "Let's pressure-cook it," he announced cheerfully.

He had me there. "I'm soft as a grape," I murmured. "Throw me the spellout."

"Okay, crowd in," he said, pulling out a document from his brief case. "See what you can make of this letter that went out from an agency the other day: 'You are absolutely right about how it figures—TV is pricing itself right out of the market. What frosts us is that . . . the only way you can go home with your skin on is to buy the stuff packaged. . . .' "

I took a deep breath. "It doesn't quite jell with me," I said. "When you glim the over-all picture, you must realize there are certain rock-bottom slants which have to be considered before the final wrap-up," I paused. "How am I doing?"

"Just fair. You are still too definite. . . . You got to housebreak it for the top brass."

"Housebreak it? That's a new one. How do you housebreak an idea?"

"You kick it around. You take a reading of the general situation to be sure that the whole picture hasn't changed. You gather the gang and spit-ball until the wrinkles are ironed out. You mother-hen it. You talk off the top of your head and the bottom of your pants. In short, you finalize it. By that time it's so thoroughly housebroken its mother wouldn't recognize it."

JOHN CROSBY IN THE *NEW YORK HERALD TRIBUNE*

Jack Kerouac declaims his verse to fellow poets

The Mystical Bohemians

The only people for me are the mad ones, the ones who are mad to live, mad to talk, mad to be saved . . . the ones who never yawn or say a commonplace thing, but burn, burn, burn like fabulous yellow roman candles exploding like spiders across the stars.

JACK KEROUAC, *ON THE ROAD*

In the mid-'50s a new group of American-bred bohemians emerged, calling themselves the Beat Generation. "Beat," according to one theory, was a contraction of "beatitude"; the Beats felt that they had been blessed with mystical powers. But many of the new bohemians had fought in the Korean war and were disillusioned with the old American dream of prosperity and conformity; for them "Beat" simply meant "beaten down."

The beatniks, as they were soon known, were an easily recognizable breed. Originally a West Coast phenomenon, they first congregated in San Francisco and in Los Angeles' scruffy Venice West. The men favored beards but wore their hair short, and their clothing—usually khaki pants, a sweater and sandals—carefully avoided any hint of flamboyance. The girls wore black leotards and no lipstick, but so much eyeshadow that people joked about their "raccoon eyes."

They spoke their own argot, mostly picked up from Negro jazz musicians and juvenile street gangs: "chick," "dig," "bug," "spade" to mean "Negro," "bread" for money and "like" as an all-purpose pause-word and qualifier. They experimented with marijuana, which they called "pot." Both sexes bundled up in flats they called "pads," furnished with no more than a guitar, a hot plate, a bare mattress and a few records and books. The records were usually of the most rarefied jazz (Miles Davis, Thelonius Monk) and the books were often about Zen, a Buddhist offshoot which taught that enlightenment could be achieved by abandoning rational, word-oriented thought. Although few Beats really understood Zen, it seemed to fit in with their longing for exotic experiences and instant inspiration.

To a nation acquiring a belated awareness of its own conformism, the rebellious life style of the new bohemians was both fascinating and repulsive. The mass media quickly exploited this ambivalence. The radio soap opera *Helen Trent* added a Beat character; Hollywood cranked out an exposé of Beat "orgies," and the big magazines treated them at best with condescension.

Amid the hubbub, Beat spokesmen carefully pointed out that they were not at all the dangerous revolutionaries that the "squares" imagined them to be. Novelist Jack Kerouac, a leading oracle of the movement, insisted: "We love everything—Bill Graham, the Big Ten, Rock and Roll, Zen, apple pie, Eisenhower—we dig it all. We're in the vanguard of the new religion."

A Beat folk singer strums a guitar in a dimly lit coffeehouse; Beats favored songs of protest—Negro blues and Depression ballads.

Lawrence Ferlinghetti stands outside his San Francisco store.

The Beat Generation not only had a distinctive life style, it also produced its own literature. The literary center was San Francisco—critics spoke of the "San Francisco Renaissance"—and headquarters was a bookstore on Columbus Avenue called City Lights (after a Chaplin film). The store's owner was Lawrence Ferlinghetti, the eye in the center of the Beat storm. A poet himself, Ferlinghetti came to San Francisco in the early '50s, after working as a *Time* magazine mail boy, serving in the Navy and studying in Paris. One of his contributions to Beat literature was the reading and recording in 1957 of his poem "Tentative Description of a Dinner To Promote The Impeachment of President Eisenhower" with Cal Tjader on drums. He also became a book publisher, starting with his own poetry and then with editions of works by a poet named Gregory Corso, and by Allen Ginsberg, the minstrel of the Beats.

Copies of Ginsberg's poem "Howl" were seized by policemen in 1957 on grounds of obscenity (a local newspaper wrote: "San Francisco Cops Don't Want No Renaissance"). But a judge ruled that "Howl" had "redeeming social importance," and the trial brought notoriety to the Beat literary movement, which reached its peak during the next two years when Jack Kerouac's novel, *On The Road,* sold half a million copies. A saga of footloose bohemians who crisscrossed the country having visions and seducing girls, the book became a Bible to young people eager to Experience Life. Samples of this and other Beat works are on pages 88-89.

Beat customers browse idly through Ferlinghetti's City Lights Bookshop. The accommodating shop even held mail for itinerant authors.

The prose and poetry of Beat writers was often undisciplined but powerful. Some typical Beat preoccupations—travel, sex, America and Oriental religion—are examined in the excerpts below.

Recently Ben Hecht said to me on TV "Why are you afraid to speak out your mind, what's wrong with this country, what is everybody afraid of?" Was he talking to me? And all he wanted me to do was speak out my mind AGAINST people, he sneeringly brought up Dulles, Eisenhower, the Pope, all kinds of people like that habitually he would sneer at with Drew Pearson, AGAINST the world he wanted, this is his idea of freedom, he calls it freedom. Who knows, my God, but that the universe is not one vast sea of compassion actually, the veritable holy honey, beneath all this show of personality and cruelty. In fact who knows but that it isn't the solitude of the oneness of the essence of everything, the solitude of the actual oneness of the unbornness of the unborn essence of everything, nay the true pure foreverhood, that big blank potential that can ray forth anything it wants from its pure store, that blazing bliss, "Mattivajrakaruna" the Transcendental Diamond Compassion! No, I want to speak FOR things, for the crucifix I speak out, for the Star of Israel I speak out, for the divinest man who ever lived who was a German (Bach) I speak out, for sweet Mohammed I speak out, for Buddha I speak out, for Lao-tse and Chuang-tse I speak out, for D. T. Suzuki I speak out . . . why should I attack what I love out of life. This is Beat. Live your lives out? Naw, LOVE your lives out. When

they come and stone you at least you won't have a glass house, just your glassy flesh.

"THE ORIGINS OF THE BEAT GENERATION" BY JACK KEROUAC

That night I found Carlo and to my amazement he told me he'd been in Central City with Dean.

"What did you do?"

"Oh, we ran around the bars and then Dean stole a car and we drove back down the mountain curves ninety miles an hour."

"I didn't see you."

"We didn't know you were there."

"Well, man, I'm going to San Francisco."

"Dean has Rita lined up for you tonight."

"Well, then, I'll put it off." I had no money. I sent my aunt an airmail letter asking her for fifty dollars and said it would be the last money I'd ask; after that she would be getting money back from me, as soon as I got that ship.

Then I went to meet Rita Bettencourt and took her back to the apartment. I got her in my bedroom after a long talk in the dark of the front room. She was a nice little girl, simple and true, and tremendously frightened of sex. I told her it was beautiful. I wanted to prove this to her. She let me prove it, but I was too impatient and proved nothing. She sighed in the dark. "What do you want out of life?" I asked, and I used to ask that all the time of girls.

"I don't know," she said. "Just wait on tables and try to get along." She yawned. I put my hand over her mouth and told her not to yawn. I tried to tell her how excited I was about life and the things we could do to-

gether; saying that, and planning to leave Denver in two days. She turned away wearily. We lay on our backs, looking at the ceiling and wondering what God had wrought when He made life so sad. We made vague plans to meet in Frisco.   ON THE ROAD BY JACK KEROUAC

America when I was seven momma took me to Communist Cell meetings they sold us garbanzos a handful per ticket a ticket costs a nickel and the speeches were free everybody was angelic and sentimental about the workers it was all so sincere you have no idea what a good thing the party was in 1935 Scott Nearing was a grand old man a real mensch Mother Bloor made me cry I once saw Israel Amter plain. Everybody must have been a spy.

America you don't really want to go to war.

America it's them bad Russians.

Them Russians them Russians and them Chinamen. And them Russians.

The Russia wants to eat us alive. The Russia's power-mad. She wants to take our cars from out our garages.

Her wants to grab Chicago. Her needs a Red Reader's Digest. Her wants our auto plants in Siberia. Him big bureaucracy running our fillingstations.

That no good. Ugh. Him make Indians learn read. Him need big black niggers. Hah. Her make us all work sixteen hours a day. Help.

America this is quite serious.

America this is the impression I get from looking in the television set.

America is this correct?

I'd better get right down to the job.

It's true I don't want to join the Army or turn lathes in precision parts factories, I'm nearsighted and psychopathic anyway.

America I'm putting my queer shoulder to the wheel.   "AMERICA" BY ALLEN GINSBERG

Should I get married? Should I be good?

Astound the girl next door with my velvet suit and faustus hood?

Don't take her to movies but to cemeteries tell all about werewolf bathtubs and forked clarinets then desire her and kiss her and all the preliminaries and she going just so far and I understanding why not getting angry saying You must feel! It's beautiful to feel!

Instead you take her in my arms lean against an old crooked tombstone

and woo her the entire night the constellations in the sky—

When she introduces me to her parents back straightened, hair finally combed, strangled by a tie, should I sit knees together on their 3rd degree sofa and not ask Where's the bathroom?

How else to feel other than I am, often thinking Flash Gordon soap—

O how terrible it must be for a young man seated before a family and the family thinking

We never saw him before! He wants our Mary Lou!

After tea and homemade cookies they ask What do you do for a living?   "MARRIAGE" BY GREGORY CORSO

Kenneth Rexroth

The elder statesman of the Beats was Kenneth Rexroth, a former
popcorn machine operator, cowboy and cab driver whose readings of poetry and prose
on San Francisco's radio station KPFA gave a hefty boost to the local literary
ferment. Rexroth, who was in his fifties and himself both a poet and a painter, interested
his younger compatriots in Oriental culture through his
translations of Chinese and Japanese verse. With iconoclastic bravado he once announced,
"I write poetry to seduce women and overthrow the capitalist system."

Jack Kerouac

*"A very unique cat—a French Canadian Hinayana Buddhist
Beat Catholic savant," was the way Allen Ginsberg described Jack Kerouac, author
of the most famous Beat novel, "On The Road." The son of French-
Canadian parents, Kerouac played football at Columbia University, served in the Navy—and
drifted about the U.S. His wanderings provided the material for
"On The Road," which he wrote in three weeks. Truman Capote's comment on Kerouac's
fever-pitch method of composition was: "It isn't writing at all—it's typing!"*

Allen Ginsberg

*The son of a poet and schoolteacher, Allen Ginsberg came
from what he once called a "Jewish left-wing atheist Russian background in Paterson,
New Jersey." After studying at Columbia University,
where he met Kerouac, Ginsberg became a book reviewer and market
research consultant. A year of psychotherapy, however, liberated him from his middle
class aspirations. Whereupon, he dashed off "Howl," the verses
that made him one of America's best-known poets.*

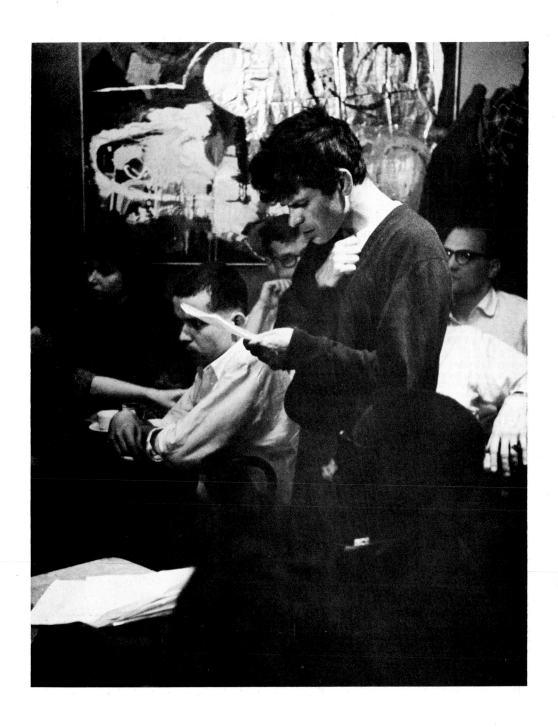

Gregory Corso

The enfant terrible of Beatdom, Corso was a puckish, tousle-haired
product of New York's slums. At 16 he was arrested for attempting, with two other
friends, to take over New York City by means of a campaign of complex
robberies coordinated with walkie-talkies; for this he was arrested and put in Clinton
Prison for three years. After his release he educated himself at the
Harvard library, wrote poetry and, when interviewed, made inscrutable comments:
"Fried shoes. Like it means nothing. Don't shoot the warthog."

Eyes of the Nation

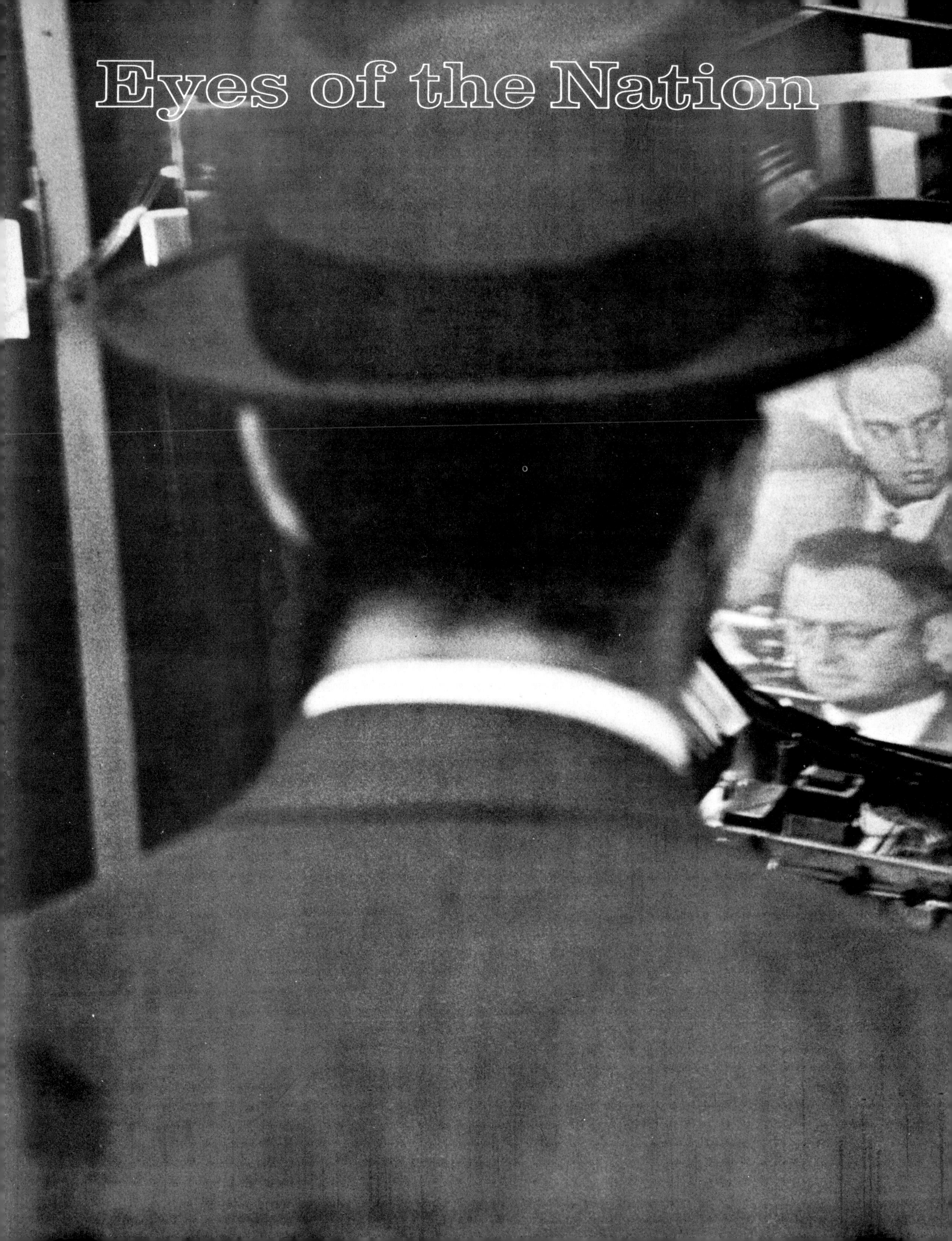

Window-shopping New Yorkers pause to watch the Army-McCarthy hearings.

The Political Circus

Sincerity is the quality that comes through on television. RICHARD M. NIXON, 1955

Does it sort out the charlatan from the statesman? Are we quite sure that Father Coughlin and Huey Long wouldn't have been bigger with the help of television?

EDWARD R. MURROW, 1952

The most enthralling television performer of the '50s was not Milton Berle or Dick Clark, but that master of bravado and showmanship, the American politician. To a vast home audience the close-up of Congressional committees and political conventions provided by television proved as fascinating as firsthand observation of politics had been in the era of the town meeting. And when the real spectaculars were on view, schools closed, department-store sales dropped and movies played to vacant houses—until the theater owners got smart and piped the political extravaganzas onto their screens.

The first significant performance was a televised road show staged by Senator Estes Kefauver and his Special Committee to Investigate Organized Crime. Before it opened in Miami in May of 1950, Kefauver was just another obscure, though quietly ambitious, legislator known to few beyond his Tennessee constituency. But as the Crime Committee swung through six major cities, playing a deadly game of question-and-answer with a Runyonesque assortment of crooks and political favor peddlers, the rustic Senator acquired a following that, said TV critic John Crosby, "even Howdy Doody might envy." By the time the climax came in New York City

(overleaf), Estes Kefauver had become perhaps the best-known American short of the President—whose office would be contested the following year.

Another shrewd politician turned the TV camera to good use 18 months later when G.O.P. Vice-Presidential nominee Richard M. Nixon, beset by charges that he had accepted improper campaign contributions, went on nationwide TV to throw himself at the mercy of the voters. Nixon's plea, though it never really dealt with the specific charges ("Pat and I have the satisfaction that every dime that we've got is honestly ours. I should say this—that Pat doesn't have a mink coat, but she does have a respectable Republican cloth coat. . ."), had such homely appeal that the voters welcomed him back aboard. Less than two years later, the kingmaking camera turned on one of its users and destroyed him, as Senator Joseph R. McCarthy *(pages 116-133)* bellowed his way to his own demise during a Senatorial investigation of charges and countercharges between him and the Secretary of the Army. Following this debacle, a television executive prophesied, "Perhaps television is going to change the one great American habit which none of us thought too much about—apathy."

A New York movie theater drops its regular Hollywood fare to pick up television's political spectacular, the Kefauver hearings.

Estes Kefauver and his dour-faced colleagues opened their New York City engagement at the drab Foley Square Federal Courthouse before some 20 million TV fans. But as Chief Counsel Rudolph Halley snapped questions at a fascinating parade of tight-lipped Mafia bosses, curvaceous molls and squirming pols *(following pages)*, the rave reviews for the show's entertainment value became mixed with some troubled queries about the effect TV might have on the whole process of government. In trying to answer one such question, Estes Kefauver himself gave unwitting proof *(bottom)* that the real answers might be a long time coming.

The opening session of the Senate Crime Investigating Committee was nothing less than a Hollywood thriller truly brought to life. The central characters could hardly have been cast to type more perfectly.

JACK GOULD, *NEW YORK TIMES* TELEVISION CRITIC

Here is the perfect combination of information and entertainment. Every bit of it is exciting stuff, and deserves all the presentation it is getting.

NEW YORK HERALD TRIBUNE

It was a great show. But was the televising of it legal? Was it ethical?

NEWSWEEK MAGAZINE

What about the rights of the witnesses who were haled before the committee and subjected to the heat, glare and public exposure of newsreels and television?

TELFORD TAYLOR, FORMER FCC OFFICIAL

Ridiculous! Nobody ever thought of me for President and certainly I never thought about it myself. I just want to be a United States Senator if I can, and if I can't be that I want to go back to Tennessee and be a country squire.

ESTES KEFAUVER

98

Committee members (from left): Charles Tobey of New Hampshire, Maryland's Herbert O'Conor, Kefauver and Counsel Halley.

The Hands of a Heavy

The heavy of the New York telecasts was dapper, grackle-voiced Frank Costello, reputedly the elder statesman of organized crime. Ironically, the TV audience did not see what the gangster looked like until photos like those above ran in the newspapers. On a lawyer's insistence that "Mr. Costello doesn't care to submit himself as a spectacle," TV cameras were forbidden to show his face during his testimony (*excerpted below*). Instead they focused on Costello's hands, which writhed more expressively than could any face as Committee Chief Counsel Rudolph Halley grilled him.

Costello's hands perform for the TV camera.

HALLEY: Now, Mr. Costello, will yo state whether or not prior to having be naturalized as a citizen you were e gaged in the illicit liquor business?
COSTELLO: I was not. I didn't sell no quor prior to '25.
HALLEY: Do you expect this committe to believe that story, Mr. Costello?
COSTELLO: I am not expecting you to b lieve anything. I know you werer going to believe anything when I fi come here. I have been prejudged.
HALLEY: What is your net worth?
COSTELLO: I refuse to answer. It mig tend to incriminate me.

HALLEY: You had an income in 1949 from George M. Levy [head of Roose-elt Raceway], $15,000. Would you mind telling the committee again what hat was for?

COSTELLO: Mr. Levy told me he was aving difficulty [with bookies] at the ace track. He asked me to help him. I ays, "Well, I can spread the propagan-a around that they're hurting you there nd you're a nice fellow." But I'm un-er the impression there was no such a hing as bookmakers there of any mount to be frightened.

KEFAUVER: [Then] you refuse to testify further? . . .

COSTELLO: Mr. Senator, I want to think of my health first. When I testify, I want to testify truthfully, and my mind don't function.

KEFAUVER: Your mind seems to be func-tioning pretty well.

COSTELLO: With all due respect to the Senators, I am not going to answer an-other question. You just said I am not under arrest, and I am going to walk out.

HALLEY (four days later): I wonder what [is] the basis of your ability to persuade politicians?

COSTELLO: Well, I can't readily explain

that, Mr. Halley. The idea is that I have been living all my life in the neighbor-hood, in Manhattan. I know them.

HALLEY: I think you have testified you haven't ever even voted; is that right?

COSTELLO: That's right.

HALLEY: You never made a political contribution?

COSTELLO: No. I am not a politician.

HALLEY: It is very difficult for me to un-derstand how you would be the man who would be able to sway the election of a Tammany leader, as you did in 1942.

COSTELLO: I know I am not a politician. I am a friend of some politicians.

101

The Queen of the Molls

The female lead on the Kefauver show was Virginia Hill Hauser, the blue-eyed ex-girlfriend of mobster "Bugsy" Siegel. To the fascination of Senator Tobey (*right*), the voluptuous Mrs. Hauser expounded freely on her lavish life-style —ostensibly financed from race-track winnings and gifts from men. But when queried about her alleged role as bagwoman for the crime syndicate, she played dumb. From her dramatic entrance (she kept the Senators waiting some minutes) to her spectacular exit (she slugged one reporter and told the rest, "You goddam bastards, I hope an atom bomb falls on every one of you"), she succeeded in upstaging everybody.

KEFAUVER: I might explain that Mrs. Hauser originally comes from Alabama, and in the South it is an old-fashioned custom for the ladies to keep the gentlemen waiting as long as they want to. . . . Now, gentlemen, let us give Mrs. Hauser time to accustom herself without too many flash bulbs.
MRS. HAUSER: Make them quit that.
KEFAUVER: All right, let's not flash any more bulbs. All right, Mr. Halley.
HALLEY: Do you think you would like to tell the committee the story of your life, insofar as it involves your financial affairs, and the contacts you may have had with known gangsters?

MRS. HAUSER: Well, I left home when I was 17, and I went to Chicago. . . . I worked for a while. Then the men I was around that gave me things, were not gangsters or racketeers or whatever you call [them]. . . .

The only time I ever got anything from them was going out and having fun, and maybe a few presents. . . . And then when I was with Ben he bought me everything.
HALLEY: You mean Ben Siegel?

SENATOR CHARLES W. TOBEY

MRS. HAUSER: Yes; he gave me some money, too, bought me a house in Florida. And I used to bet horses. . . .
HALLEY: Do you remember how much you earned by wagering in 1948?
MRS. HAUSER: No. I don't even—I didn't earn anything in 1948 because I wasn't here.
HALLEY: Well, you paid a tax of $3,000, so you must have earned something.
MRS. HAUSER: No. They gave me some back. I don't know about those things.
HALLEY: Well, the committee has been a little troubled because you lived very well and you apparently have been able to simply say what you think you earned in a rough round figure, without giving details, and don't seem to have taken the trouble of accounting to Uncle Sam the way the rest of us do.
MRS. HAUSER: Well then, he'll have to take care of that, won't he?
HALLEY: Uncle Sam?
MRS. HAUSER: Yes.
HALLEY: Well, maybe he will.
MRS. HAUSER: Well, that's all right, sure. I don't blame him. . . .
HALLEY: Have you ever known anybody in the narcotics traffic in Mexico?
MRS. HAUSER: Well, since I've been going to Mexico a lot of people have approached me and tried to give me those things. One fellow come one time

and said he had a lot of H. and —which I don't know what it was, ar he told me it was heroin and cocaine. told him to get out of the house. . . .
HALLEY: Mrs. Hauser, are you real not in any position to give this comm tee any of the details you must ha heard about the business of Siegel, Adonis?
MRS. HAUSER: But I never knew any thing about their business. They didr tell me about their business. Why wou they tell me?
HALLEY: The reason I ask you is tha you seem to have a great deal of abili to handle financial affairs.
MRS. HAUSER: Who, me?
HALLEY: You seem to have taken ver good care of your own finances.
MRS. HAUSER: I take care of myself.
HALLEY: It seems impossible that yo wouldn't know, for instance, who the associates were.
MRS. HAUSER: Why didn't you ask peo ple? I was around with my own friend I was never around with his friends.
HALLEY: Who were the people who hun around the Flamingo [a Las Vegas clul which Siegel owned]?
MRS. HAUSER: I was at the Flamingo o a lot of times, people didn't even know was there. I didn't even go out. In th first place I had hay fever. I was allergi to the cactus. . . .
HALLEY: Did [Joe Adonis] ever talk an politics in front of you?
MRS. HAUSER: Politics is something don't know anything about.
HALLEY: You never heard that discusse by him or Costello?
MRS. HAUSER: I never discussed politic with anybody.
HALLEY: You just didn't want to knov anything?
MRS. HAUSER: No, sir. I didn't want t know anything about anybody.

Garishly swathed in silver-blue mink and obviously enjoying her moment in the limelight, gangland's femme fatale grins provocatively.

A Bunch of the Boys

Following star witnesses like Costello and Mrs. Hauser, a sizable cast of supporting characters came on camera. Heading this picturesque rogues' gallery was New York City's beefy, ruddy-faced water supply commissioner, James J. Moran *(below)*, a close political crony of former Mayor O'Dwyer.

HALLEY: Did you ever . . . receive any campaign contributions?
MORAN: Well, it is barely possible . . .
HALLEY: Do you know Louis Weber [a convicted numbers racket operator]?
MORAN: I do.
HALLEY: Was he also a frequent visitor at your office?
MORAN: It is possible that Weber came in my office three times during that period. . . . And if you want to know what I ever got from Louis Weber, he came in around Eastertime with a little bottle of perfume that he gave me, that I thought was, well, a damn nice thing for anybody to do.

FRANK ERICKSON

To learn more about bookmaking at city tracks, the Senators called a convicted bookie, Frank Erickson. Bald, round-cheeked and benign-looking as a monk, Erickson was notably entertaining—if uninformative—about his employment.

HALLEY: What is your business?
ERICKSON: My business—I have no business; I am in jail.
HALLEY: What was your business prior to being convicted? Were you a bookmaker?
ERICKSON: I refuse to answer on the grounds it might intend to criminate me.
HALLEY: You went to the schools of New York?
ERICKSON: Yes.
HALLEY: How far did your education progress?
ERICKSON: About the fourth grade.
HALLEY: And then what did you do? Did you go out to work?
ERICKSON: I refuse to answer on the grounds it might tend to incriminate me.

One of New York's top gangland [offi]cials was sleek Joe Adonis *(below)*, [who] also refused to talk about busin[ess.] Small wonder: An ex-bootlegger [who] had wriggled out of charges of ex[tor]tion, kidnapping and assault, Joe [is] currently under indictment for runn[ing] a gambling empire in New Jersey.

HALLEY: What is your present busine[ss?]
ADONIS: I don't have any at the ti[me.]
HALLEY: Have you disassociated y[our]self from the Automotive Conveya[nce] Company?
ADONIS: I decline to answer that q[ues]tion on the ground that it might ten[d to] incriminate me.
HALLEY: You just won't talk about y[our] connection with the Ford Company?
ADONIS: Well, if you want to put it [that] way.
HALLEY: What other legitimate occu[pa]tions have you had in the last five ye[ars?]
ADONIS: I decline to answer on the sa[me] grounds.

JAMES J. MORAN

JOE AD[ONIS]

hat with the Fifth Amendment pleas
witnesses like Erickson and Adonis,
e Senators had a hard time pinning
wn gangsters on specific crimes. Then
became apparent that gang chief
ank Costello had committed perjury.
ntrary to Costello's sworn testimony,
seemed that a former telephone work-
named James F. McLaughlin had

JAMES F. MC LAUGHLIN

een paid to warn the gangster—and a
ony—if the law tapped their phones.

ALLEY: Did Costello ask you to do
nything for him?
IcLAUGHLIN: Costello asked me to
ok over his telephone.
ALLEY: How much did he pay you?

IcLAUGHLIN: Well, it varied. At times
hen I met him he would give me $50,
00.
ALLEY: Did you ever check the lines
r any officials of New York City?
cLAUGHLIN: Yes, I did. . . . That was
ayor O'Dwyer.

The crime syndicate ran a rub-out op-
eration called Murder Inc. The chief
killer was Albert Anastasia, ostensibly
a stevedore. Albert's brother Anthony
was asked to explain how the gunman
lived so high on a dockhand's pay.

JOSEPH NELLIS, ASSISTANT COUNSEL:
What was your brother's salary?
ANASTASIA: I believe it was a hundred
or a hundred and a quarter, something
like that—or ninety.
NELLIS: A hundred and a quarter a
week?
ANASTASIA: Something like that. I don't
want to lie to you, sir.
NELLIS: Did you ever hear that the
house at Palisades that belongs to your
brother is worth in excess of $70,000?
ANASTASIA: No, sir.
NELLIS: And his income, as far as you
know, is $125 a week?
ANASTASIA: I am not sure, sir, whatever
it was. I no want to lie to you, if it was
90 or 100 or 125 or 110.

ANTHONY ANASTASIA

FRANK C. BALS

It was obvious to everyone that mob-
sters like Adonis and Costello could not
operate without tacit cooperation from
the local police. To find out about corruption among New York City's finest,
the committee questioned Frank C.
Bals, retired Seventh Deputy Police
Commissioner, whose main talent as a
cop had apparently been his ability to
look the other way at the right time.

JAMES WALSH, ASSISTANT COUNSEL:
Did you cause any investigation to be
made of Frank Costello?
BALS: I did not.
WALSH: Joe Adonis?
BALS: No, sir.
WALSH: And does [Adonis] have a rep-
utation for controlling the rackets in
Brooklyn?
BALS: He has a reputation for being con-
nected with them.
WALSH: Did you attempt to ascertain
what that connection was?
BALS: No, I didn't.

Just Plain Bill

The finale of the New York hearings was provided by the City's silver-haired former mayor, William O'Dwyer. Accused of appointing friends of Mafia lieutenants to certain city posts, O'Dwyer huffily retorted, "There are things you have to do politically if you want to get cooperation." But his grandstand defense crumbled when an official of the firemen's union testified that O'Dwyer had once handed him a $10,000 bribe.

TOBEY: When you went to see [Costello], you were conscious of the fact that he was a gangster, weren't you?
O'DWYER: I was conscious that he had a reputation for being an outstanding bookmaker. . . . You have bookmaking all over the country. They say there is a lot of it in New Hampshire, too.
TOBEY: Well, we haven't a Costello. . . .
O'DWYER: I wonder who the bookmakers in Bretton Woods support

for public office.
TOBEY: Well, I will tell you one th[ing] they did not support, and he is talki[ng] to you now.
O'DWYER: Would you like to go in[to] that?
TOBEY: Yes, I would. I challenge yo[u]
O'DWYER: Well, I am under oath, a[nd] you aren't, sir.
TOBEY: I will take the oath right now[. I] hate a four-flusher.

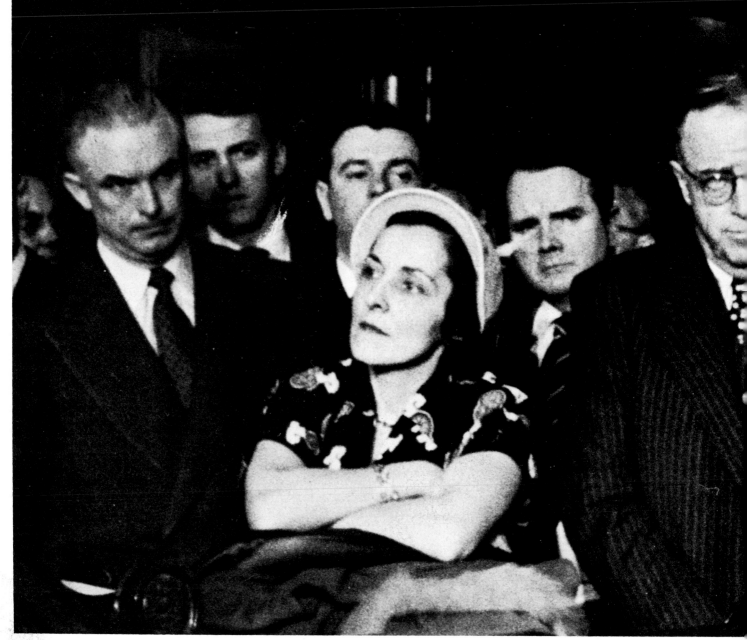

Surrounded by microphones and intent spectators, ex-mayor William O'Dwyer defends his administration against charges of corruption.

Under the Big Top

When the Republicans and then the Democrats
convened at Chicago in the summer of 1952 to pick
Presidential candidates, the bulging eye
of television for the first time brought the delegates'
shrieking, foot-stomping, sign-waving antics
live to a national audience of fascinated TV watchers.

Americans had never seen anything quite like the 1952
Presidential nominating conventions. In 1948 television
had been too limited to show much of the action. But in
July 1952 the three major networks shipped 30 tons of
equipment and more than a thousand workers to Chicago's International Amphitheater; and when Republican National Chairman Guy Gabrielson whacked down
his opening gavel, 70 million Americans saw him do it.

Over the next three weeks of conventioneering, the
people had ringside seats to a first-class political war as
the G.O.P. fought to decide whether Dwight Eisenhower or Robert Taft would be its nominee; and the show
was every bit as good when the Democrats threw over a
succession of hopefuls while Adlai Stevenson wavered.

Televiewers saw the implied threat of patronage to
be given or withheld in every down beat of Tom Dewey's
stubby forefinger as he polled the New York delegation
for Eisenhower votes. And they saw him take a dam-
aging shot from Taft-backer Everett Dirksen, who
admonished: "Tom Dewey, we followed you before and
you took us down the road to defeat. And, don't do this
to us again." They watched with amusement as the camera caught G.O.P. Committeewoman Mrs. Charles
Howard slipping out of her shoes before stepping to the
microphone. They saw a dazed Kefauver face the real-
ization that he was out of the running. They heard the
eloquent, witty Stevenson introduce his running mate,
John Sparkman, as a prime piece of "political live-
stock." And they enjoyed a disarming moment of
frankness from an exhausted announcer battling his
way through a crowd after Ike's nomination: "We're
waiting for the General now. We don't know when he'll
come out. And frankly, I don't care any more."

A favorite with televiewers, CBS convention commentator Walter Cronkite drew criticism from his bosses, who said he "talked too much."

Ex-President Hoover castigates "dishonor in high places."

The G.O.P. Opens the Show.

Pennsylvania Governor John Fine loudly demands a hearing.

A gaggle of Eisenhower girls gathers underneath ruffled parasols.

Tom Dewey supports Ike.

MacArthur denounces the Democrats.

California Governor Earl Warren's three daughters applaud a speech.

A delegate signals for a vote on the seating credentials.

Ike's floor manager Lodge grabs a bite.

Ohio's Bender and Dirksen of Illinois plump for Taft.

The Democrats Pick Their Man

F.D.R.'s widow is called "First Lady of the World."

Vice-Presidential nominee Sparkman salutes the crowd.

Mavericks in the Texas delegation noisily protest the pro-Stevenson party line.

A coonskin-capped Tennessean whoops for Kefauver.

Massachusetts' J. F. Kennedy

The convention cheers the rejected Vice-Presidential candidate Barkley.

South Carolina's Jimmy Byrnes hammers home a point.

Democratic war-horse Harry Truman fingers the new Presidential candidate, Adlai Stevenson.

Flanked by smiling wives, Ike and Vice-Presidential candidate Nixon kick off the campaign with a buoyant, hands-raised victory signal.

A Couple of Joes

For 36 days in 1954, a struggle for power
raged in Washington. Technically, it was just
a Senate subcommittee hearing on a dispute
between Republican Senator Joseph R. McCarthy and
the U.S. Army—but at stake was the integrity
of the American political system. As the two sides
set upon each other with charges and countercharges,
20 million Americans watched on television.

When, on the 30th day of the Army-McCarthy hearings, the end came for Senator Joseph R. McCarthy, he had just finished another harangue. His black-stubbled jowls were spread in the familiar wolfish grin as he awaited the usual tribute of applause. Instead the people—his people—who were jammed against the marble columns and crimson curtains of the Senate Caucus Room, applauded his enemy, another Joe named Welch. McCarthy seemed puzzled and suddenly alone. He held his palms up in bafflement and said: "What did I do?"

He had done nothing different, really, from what he had been doing for the past 1,700 days. During that time, the Wisconsin Republican turned Washington upside down. He had set up a retinue of civil-servant informants, exercised a virtual veto over State Department personnel and U.S. foreign policy, demoralized the Voice of America, driven from Washington four Senators who opposed his methods, charged two Presidents with treason, wrung sobs from the Secretary of the Army and added his name to the language as a symbol of persecution. All told, McCarthy had probably come as close to wrecking the U.S. political system as had any man in the previous century.

The era of McCarthyism began the night of February 9, 1950, in the old McLure Hotel in Wheeling, West Virginia, where the Senator had flown to address the local Republican Lincoln Day dinner. In the four and a half previous years—since the end of World War II—Communism had changed from ally to menace; and the United States, an essentially insular nation, had suddenly been thrust into leadership of a complex, contentious world. Nothing seemed to go right for the new leaders. Communists had taken over Czechoslovakia and Hungary and had conquered China; they had exploded an A-bomb and encircled West Berlin with a blockade. Americans were angry and bewildered. What had gone wrong? Had the U.S. been sold out? There were those who thought so. "Traitors in the high councils in our own government," said an ambitious California Congressman named Richard Nixon, "have made sure that the deck is stacked on the Soviet side."

The House Un-American Activities Committee began to seek out the traitors. To the astonishment of some Americans and the dismay of all, it found some. A number of government employees who were Communists or Communist sympathizers apparently had fed highly confidential information to the Russians. Several of them were convicted of various crimes in the aftermath of the committee hearings—notably a one-time State Department official named Alger Hiss. There were not many such cases. But there were enough to lend a semblance of reasonableness to the growing Red scare.

It was at this moment that Joseph McCarthy stepped forward, claiming he had the names of live Reds, busy undermining the government right now. Holding aloft a document, he told his West Virginia audience: "I have here in my hand a list of 205 names known to the Secretary of State as being members of the Communist Party and who nevertheless are still working and shaping the policy of the State Department." Next day, when he spoke in Denver, the 205 Communists had become 205 "security risks;" the day after, in Salt Lake City, the 205 security risks changed to "57 card-carrying Communists"; 10 days later in the Senate the 57 Communists became "81 cases."

The fact was that there were no names at all. What McCarthy held in his hand that night was a three-year-old letter from former Secretary of State James Byrnes; it informed a Congressman that permanent tenure for 205 unnamed State employees might be denied on various grounds, including drunkenness. Six months after the Wheeling speech, a hastily convened Senate subcommittee concluded that the Senator had perpetrated a "fraud and a hoax." But no one was listening; an anxious nation was launched on a four-year binge of hysteria and character assassination. Americans needed to lay blame and Joseph McCarthy had offered them some simple, understandable targets.

In a later speech McCarthy conjured up more frightening arithmetic: "We've been losing to international Communism at the rate of 100 million people a year." Then, ominously: "Perhaps we should examine the background of the men who have done the planning, and let the American people decide whether . . . we've lost because of stumbling, fumbling idiocy, or because they planned it that way."

Millions of Americans listened as McCarthy, under protection of Senatorial immunity, then began naming names. He called Secretary of State Dean Acheson "The Red Dean." He described Far East expert Owen Lattimore as the "top Russian espionage agent in the U.S." and charged that U.S. Ambassador to the U.N. Philip Jessup was "preaching the Communist Party line." Besides name-calling McCarthy quickly proved that he could break people. Millard Tydings, a conservative Maryland Democrat who had chaired the 1950 Senate subcommittee that branded McCarthy's Wheeling charges a "hoax," ran for reelection later that year. McCarthy was waiting. He had a composite photograph put together purporting to show Tydings talking amiably with former U.S. Communist chief Earl Browder, saturated Maryland with copies and was widely credited with defeating the Senator's bid for a sure fifth term. He also took the scalps of other Senators who got in his way, among them Senate Democratic floor leader Scott Lucas of Illinois, Ernest MacFarland of Arizona and William Benton and Raymond Baldwin of Connecticut. He accused the Voice of America of deliberately constructing two radio transmitters where they would be ineffective; M.I.T. and RCA experts later disproved McCarthy but by then one engineer who had been in-

volved had committed suicide. McCarthy encouraged fanatical anti-Communist government workers to leak confidential documents to him and grinned that he commanded a "Loyal American Underground."

This was McCarthyism, the exploitation of a nation's fears, a brutal attack on Americans with divergent views, and it became an overriding fact of American life. Although in four years McCarthy was unable to offer legal support for a single charge, nevertheless people were stampeded. "McCarthy may have something," said Massachusetts Congressman John F. Kennedy. Truman's Attorney General, J. Howard McGrath, in 1952 ordered six detention camps readied to incarcerate alleged spies and saboteurs.

To Republicans, who had been out of power for nearly 20 years, McCarthy seemed to be a godsend: The charges he was throwing at alleged Communists invariably wound up besmirching Democrats. In the Senate cloakroom, John Bricker, the 1944 G.O.P. Vice-Presidential candidate, said: "Joe, you're a dirty son of a bitch but there are times when you've got to have a son of a bitch around, and this is one of them." The usually high-minded Senator Robert Taft, his eye on the '52 Presidential nomination, told McCarthy: "If one case doesn't work, try another." McCarthy himself, suddenly propelled from backwoods nonentity to party luminary, was cynical about his new fame and power. To a woman who asked him at a March cocktail party "When did you discover Communism?" he gaily answered, "Why, about two and a half months ago." But he cherished every ounce of his new status. He had, in fact, been striving for it almost all his 41 years.

Joseph McCarthy was that classic American figure, the poor farm boy battling to escape the harsh, sterile dirt farm of his youth, determined to get his share of the American dream. As a youth Joe had tried to make it chicken farming, then tried being a chain-grocery manager. At 20 he quit, crammed four years of high school into one and got into Marquette University, where he made ends meet by jockeying a gas pump, playing poker and coaching boxing. He moved ahead, twisting and turning. At college he switched from engineering to law, in politics he ran for local office as a Democrat and lost, then switched to Republican and won, becoming a Wisconsin circuit court judge. After World War II he made it to the United States Senate.

McCarthy's first three years in the Senate marked him as simply another ambitious young legislator —somewhat prone to use the knee and the elbow, but always with a smile, a wisecrack, the friendly, open look of the American boy playing the get-ahead game, certain everyone understood he meant nothing personal. Joe wasn't mad at anybody, he was just going places. He briefly supported the interests of the sugar and soft drink industries and acquired the Washington nickname of "The Pepsi-Cola Kid," then served the housing interests and got himself called "Water Boy of the Real Estate Lobby." To please his German-American constituents he intruded into a Senate investigation of 43 Nazi SS men who had confessed to murdering captured GIs during the Battle of the Bulge and so helped muddy the proceedings of the "Malmédy Massacre" hearings that the murderers were spared. It kept him busy, but it didn't seem to be getting him anywhere.

Then, in Wheeling that February evening as the '50s began, Joe finally caught hold of a star and started his meteoric climb. Within a few months he was describing President Truman and Acheson as "the Pied Pipers of the Politburo," adding of the President: "The son of a bitch ought to be impeached." He called General George C. Marshall, Chief of the U.S. General Staff in World War II and later Secretary of State, "a man steeped in falsehood," and "an instrument of the Soviet conspiracy." This was going a bit far, and Dwight Eisenhower bristled with rage at the slur on his former commander. Nevertheless, in July of 1952, the same Republican Presidential convention that nominated Ike invited McCarthy to address the delegates; convention chairman Walter Hallanan hailed the Senator, who had been a rear-echelon leatherneck in World War II, as "Wiscon-

sin's Fighting Marine"; and Joe strode through the Chicago International Amphitheater, to be cheered as the band blared "From the Halls of Montezuma." Later, when Ike stumped Wisconsin, he dropped from his prepared speech a paragraph extolling Marshall.

Although in all this time only a handful of Republicans had ever taken on McCarthy (Senator Margaret Chase Smith had attacked him in 1950 with the words: "I do not want to see the Republican Party ride to political victory on the Four Horsemen of Calumny—fear, ignorance, bigotry and smear"), many Republican and independent anti-McCarthyites believed in 1952 that only the G.O.P. could end his career. "McCarthyism would disappear overnight if Eisenhower were elected," predicted the *Washington Post*. And indeed the day after Ike's victory, McCarthy said, "Now it will be unnecessary for me to conduct a one-man campaign to expose Communists." Senator Taft commented: "We've got McCarthy where he can't do any harm." But in a few weeks the bad boy was back, doing business at the same stand, this time taking on not only Communists and Democrats, but the G.O.P. itself.

To Eisenhower's astonishment and anger, Joe charged the Administration with sending "perfumed notes" to friendly powers who were profiting from "blood trade" with Red China. He threatened to investigate the CIA. He fought Ike's nomination of Charles Bohlen as Ambassador to Moscow, claiming that the State Department's personnel chief, Scott McLeod, had not cleared Bohlen. (This incident disclosed an agreement by incoming Secretary of State John Foster Dulles to put McCarthy's friend McLeod in charge of hiring and firing. Dulles cleared all appointments with McLeod, who cleared them with McCarthy.) The Senator finally let the Bohlen appointment through, but only on the understanding that the Administration would make no further objectionable appointments.

By now Joseph McCarthy seemed to be the second most powerful man in the country. "The Senate," said the *Christian Science Monitor*, "is afraid of him." So, apparently, was everyone else. One day in 1953 a U.S. diplomat just back from abroad was handed a note by a State Department colleague: "Let's get out of here. This place is wired." They walked and the Washington official said: "You just don't know what's happened here. People don't talk at staff meetings any more. They've discovered that an opinion which is nonconformist is reported." Even Eisenhower was reluctant to throw down any challenge. Privately Ike described McCarthy as "a lawless man." But when Ike's advisers pleaded that the President strike down this apparently ungovernable menace, Ike declined. "I just will not," he said. "I refuse to get into the gutter with that guy."

There seemed no stopping McCarthy. He boasted: "McCarthyism is Americanism with its sleeve rolled." He gloried in being himself: the poor kid from the wrong side of the tracks who had fought his way up, who was going to teach the snobs a thing or two. "McCarthyism," wrote critic Peter Viereck, "is the revenge of the noses that for 20 years of fancy parties were pressed against the outside window pane." The Wisconsin Senator had tapped into one of the universal, recurring themes in American life: the antagonism between the uppitty, dudish, big-city smart alecks and the rough and ready, independent, true-blue Americans from the backwoods. "It is not the less fortunate . . . who have been selling this nation out," he cried, "but rather those who have had all the benefits—the finest homes, the finest college educations, and the finest jobs in government. The bright young men who are born with silver spoons in their mouths are the worst."

As 1954 began, McCarthy took on the biggest game of all. He amended his slam at the Democrats, "Twenty years of treason," and charged "Twenty-one years of treason." The meaning was amply clear. A few months later, when a *New York Herald Tribune* reporter attempted to question Ike about McCarthy, the President "clenched his hands together and . . . declining to talk, and nearly speechless with emotion, . . . strode from the room. His eyes appeared moist." As of that moment, the Senator seemed to have the whole country in his pocket.

But blinded by his success, he had already begun to overreach. In October 1953 he had launched an investigation of the U.S. Army, the pillar of order, and the heart of Ike's heart. The subject was supposed subversion at the Fort Monmouth Army Signal Corps Center. In January 1954 he went even further, questioning the routine promotion at Camp Kilmer of a leftish captain, Irving Peress. McCarthy inflamed the country with charges of "Communist coddling." He savaged Kilmer's commander, General Ralph Zwicker, a World War II combat hero: "You are a disgrace to the uniform. You're not fit to be an officer. You're ignorant." He bulldozed Army Secretary Robert Stevens, a well-bred, Yale-educated industrialist who tried fitfully to protect his men but ended in abject surrender, even offering McCarthy and his staff the use of his personal membership in New York's posh Merchant's Club (the bills to be sent to Stevens). Hounded and exhausted, the Army Secretary, sobbing over the telephone, offered to resign.

The confrontation finally came to a head when the Army drafted one of McCarthy's staff, a handsome young fellow named G. David Schine who pretended to a profound knowledge of Communism. Schine had been taken onto Joe's staff at the insistence of McCarthy's counsel and brain-truster, Roy Cohn, one of the most lordly 27-year-olds since Alexander of Macedon. Cohn drove the Army to distraction trying to wangle a commission for his crony. He phoned Stevens and Army Counsel John Adams innumerable times to argue for Schine. Some days he threatened to "wreck the Army."

And now, at last, even Ike had apparently had enough of McCarthyism; in any event he allowed his staff to move. On January 21, 1954, chief Presidential aide Sherman Adams secretly instructed the Army to prepare a brief to prove that McCarthy and Cohn were trying to blackmail it into commissioning Schine by threatening further investigations if it did not. In March the Army made the charges public. McCarthy countercharged that the Army was using David Schine as a hostage, in order to inhibit his investigation of the military.

On April 22, as a battery of TV cameras zeroed in on the Caucus Room *(right)*, a Senate subcommittee chaired by Republican Karl Mundt began to probe the conflicting charges. Superficially the hearings seemed to be a typical McCarthy performance. The Wisconsin Senator devastated the Army Secretary on the witness stand, threw the meetings into confusion with repeated cries of "point of order" and on the whole seemed to be well ahead in the early scoring. But there was one difference. Now and then, as some 20 million televiewers listened with fascination to the exchanges of dialogue *(following pages)*, an elderly, bow-tied gentleman who had been appointed special counsel for the Army would intervene gently, softly, quizzically. Slowly he began to emerge as a major figure in the hearings.

Unlike Joseph McCarthy, Joseph Welch did little to bring to mind the hardscrabble Midwest farm country where he was born and raised. At age 24 Welch had entered Harvard on a law school scholarship and he had stayed on in Massachusetts, becoming, as converts often do, more Boston than the Bostonians. At 63, Welch had all the attributes of the Beacon Hill brahmin—the large, old-fashioned bow ties, the rumpled coat, the colonial house, the assured, lifelong Republicanism, the partnership in the old, conservative law firm of Hale & Dorr, where, alone of 19 partners, he worked at an old-fashioned stand-up desk.

Joe Welch had as obviously made his arrangements with society as Joe McCarthy had not, and Welch fought with all the knowledge, guile and toughness that had made that society to begin with and that had preserved it ever since. The duel between the two men quickly cap-

PRIVATE G. DAVID SCHINE

tured national attention. Welch, his manner soft, his mind sharp, cut deftly at McCarthy's case; McCarthy roared and raged back. On the 30th day, the climax occurred, unexpectedly and dramatically.

Welch was questioning Cohn, needling him, asking why Cohn had not stormed at the Army to proclaim that Communists were flourishing at Fort Monmouth. Cohn, trying to answer, began stumbling, sounding indeed as witnesses had sounded in front of McCarthy—seeking words, pleading bad memory: "I don't remember . . . I don't know whether . . ." As Welch bore in, McCarthy, squirming as his side took the sort of punishment he usually enjoyed administering, interrupted. It was fairly well known that when Welch became the special Army counsel, he had considered using as an aide a young lawyer named Fred Fisher from his own firm. On learning, however, that Fisher had once been a member of the National Lawyer's Guild, a pro-Communist organization, Welch, to avoid making an issue of him, had sent Fisher home. Now the furious McCarthy lost all discretion and lunged after Fisher before the subcommittee and the TV audience. He went on and on, reviling Fisher for no reason relevant to the hearings.

At last Welch had had enough; suddenly he turned on McCarthy. His honest, emotional indignation *(page 130)* was in sharp contrast with his usual calm demeanor, and even more so with McCarthy's brutality, coarseness and irresponsibility. This contrast was stamped indelibly on the mind of the nation. When Welch had finished speaking, he walked away into the corridor, as though McCarthy were unclean. The next day, front pages all over the nation showed the two Joes: McCarthy smiling as he savaged Fred Fisher, and Welch weeping quietly, as if for his country.

A seven-man Senate subcommittee (left side of table) hears the dispute between the U.S. Army and Joe McCarthy (far end of table).

Army Secretary Stevens testifies as Counsel Welch looks on.

McCarthy and Cohn exchange whispers.

STEVENS: *What I had in mind was to try to
convey to the committee, in probably rather tired language—*
MCCARTHY: *Yes.*
STEVENS: *—the idea that in carrying out
this job and always resolving doubts in favor
of the American people, that at the same
time we ought not to be unfair
or work hardships on individuals unnecessarily.*
MCCARTHY: *That is a fine sentiment . . .
Mr. Welch, please, I think the Secretary
is intelligent enough to listen
to this without your whispering in his ear.*

MCCARTHY: *Mr. Chairman?*

CHAIRMAN MUNDT: *Senator, may I suggest, if you are going to . . .*

MCCARTHY: *An important point of personal privilege.*

CHAIRMAN MUNDT: *Just a minute.*

MCCARTHY: *No, Mr. Chairman. This very vicious smear must be answered now.*

CHAIRMAN MUNDT: *The Chair feels that if you feel that it is so important . . .*

MCCARTHY: *I think as a point of privilege, I should . . .*

CHAIRMAN MUNDT: *There is no question . . .*

MCCARTHY: *I am glad we are on television. I think the millions of people can see how low a man can sink. I repeat, I think they can see how low an alleged man can sink. He has been asked to come here before the Committee and give the information he has . . .*

CHAIRMAN MUNDT: *The Chair recognizes Senator Symington.*

MCCARTHY: *A point of personal privilege. . . . I ask that Mr. Symington be requested, in all decency, to take this stand.*

SYMINGTON: *I would like to say . . .*

MCCARTHY: *Why don't you say that under oath?*

SYMINGTON: *Can I proceed without interruption?*

MCCARTHY: *Mr. Chairman?*

CHAIRMAN MUNDT: *A point of order?*

MCCARTHY: *Yes, a point of order. . . .*

CHAIRMAN MUNDT: *The Chair believes that it is not a point of order.*

MCCARTHY: *It is a request of the Chair.*

CHAIRMAN MUNDT: *It is not a point of order.*

MCCARTHY: *I think this is a matter of personal privilege.*

CHAIRMAN MUNDT: *Very well. A point of personal privilege.*

McCarthy bores in on the attack.

Roy Cohn testifies before the Committee.

WELCH: *When you find there are Communists and possible spies*
in a place like Monmouth, you must be alarmed, aren't you? I don't want
the sun to go down while they are still in there.
Will you not, before the sun goes down, give those names to the FBI?
COHN: *Mr. John Edgar Hoover and his men know a lot better*
than I. . . . I do not propose to tell the FBI how to run its shop.
WELCH: *All I am suggesting is that we just nudge them a little.*
COHN: *Surely, we want them out as fast as possible, sir.*
WELCH: *May I add my small voice, sir, and say whenever you know about*
a subversive or a Communist or a spy, please hurry.

Army Counsel Welch questions a witness.

MCCARTHY: *I think we should tell Mr. Welch that he has in his law firm a young man named Fisher who has been for a number of years a member of an organization named as the legal bulwark of the Communist Party. . . . Mr. Welch, I just felt that I had a duty to respond to your urgent request that before sundown, when we know of anyone serving the Communist cause, we let the agency know. . . . I have been rather bored with your phony requests to Mr. Cohn here that he personally get every Communist out of government before sundown.*

McCarthy rises to a point as Welch listens grimly.

Welch speaks out.

WELCH: *Until this moment, Senator, I think I never really gauged your cruelty or your recklessness. Fred Fisher is starting what looks to be a brilliant career with us. Little did I dream you could be so reckless and so cruel as to do an injury to that lad. I fear he shall always bear a scar needlessly inflicted by you.... Let us not assassinate this lad further, Senator. You have done enough. Have you no sense of decency, sir, at long last? Have you left no sense of decency?*

Cohn looks anxiously at a silent McCarthy.

Requiem for a Joe

The McCarthy spell was broken. The nation that had urged him on now saw him in full view as he really was, and was repelled. On September 1, 1954, the Mundt subcommittee reported its findings on the Army-McCarthy hearings: The Republican majority exonerated the Senator; the Democratic minority condemned him. But far more significantly, on the day before, new hearings had begun to determine whether McCarthy should be censured. Suddenly legislators who had lived in fear of Joe McCarthy rose up in anger. A leading Republican bluntly told Cohn: "We can't strike out this time. Unless we get rid of your boy, he's going to be a mighty big thorn in our sides." This was for keeps.

On December 2, McCarthy was condemned by a vote of 67 to 22. Die-hards still urged McCarthy to resume his battle, but the Wisconsin Senator knew the reality. No, he said, and then added a leatherneck phrase, it would be "like shovelling garbage against the tide."

Senator Joseph McCarthy strode for two more years through the Senate corridors, but it was a ghost performing. When he knew there were photographers around, he would drop into hearings and ask a few questions, some incoherent. But the photographers were not interested, so he would wander dispiritedly home, where he would sit bewildered, drinking heavily and talking endlessly about the past.

There were still a few peaks among the valleys for McCarthy. One night he rose on a TV show and, with a trace of the old fire, called Presidential aide Sherman Adams "a pinhead." But it was a shot in the gathering gloom. His despair darkened. He took to rising late and to staying home from the office. He spent days watching TV soap operas and staring into the fire. His drinking problem got worse. On May 2, 1957, his liver ravaged by alcohol, McCarthy died. The commentary that followed his death *(excerpted below)* ranged from sympathetic to cruel. Perhaps the cruelest cut of all had been made some time before by Dwight Eisenhower, as Joe's power was waning. Ike asked had the fellows heard about McCarthyism; now it was called McCarthywasm.

I got off the train and instantly wired my sympathy to the widow. McCarthy was so controversial a figure that I think only time can decide what is his place in history. I think it would be presumptuous of me to say what that place will be or should be. Early in the hearings I had some pleasant moments with him and later some flashes of high anger. But I did not hate him. If you quote me on that, please add that I'm not good at hating any man.
JOSEPH WELCH, COMMENTING ON SENATOR JOSEPH MC CARTHY'S DEATH

Senator McCarthy was a patriotic American and a determined opponent of Communists. And because of that every "liberal" commentator lost no opportunity to vilify him. The White House palace guard plotted his ruin.

The President singled him out for studied insults. No man in public life was ever persecuted and maligned because of his beliefs as was Senator McCarthy.
EDITORIAL IN THE *CHICAGO TRIBUNE*

If he had been a Hitler he might have burned down the Senate. Being McCarthy, he buckled before respectable and official opinion. He shared its view that he didn't have much of a future. . . . McCarthy, though a demon himself, was not a man possessed by demons . . . he lacked the most necessary and awesome of demagogic gifts—a belief in the sacredness of his own mission . . . It was the lack of conviction that made McCarthy vulnerable; he was a cynic.
SENATOR JOE MC CARTHY BY RICHARD ROVERE, 1959

"I Can't Do This To Me!"

Music

A rock singer wrestles with his guitar.

From Pop to Rock

Ladies and gentlemen, I'd like to do a song now, that tells a little story, that really makes a lot of sense—"Awopbopaloobop—alopbamboom! Tutti-frutti! All rootie! Tutti-frutti! All rootie!"

ELVIS PRESLEY, 1956

Ever since the middle of the 1940s, the average age of record-buyers had been dropping fast. But in the early years of the '50s that average age had not yet skidded into the teens; the typical record-store customer was in his early twenties, a so-called young adult. To suit his taste, most popular music was still bland and "sophisticated." The top male stars of the period were smooth crooners like Eddie Fisher ("O My Pa-Pa"), Harry Belafonte ("Jamaica Farewell") and Perry Como, who ambled with antiseptic amiability through his Saturday evening TV show murmuring nice-guy ballads. Females were usually sleek jazz stylists like Peggy Lee, Lena Horne and Julie London. Everything about these stars was grown-up and polished, and the songs of the period were lushly orchestrated hunks of pure romance. About the wildest thing happening was Rosemary Clooney performing bouncy little novelty tunes.

But while the grownups were dozing to Mario Lanza and Tony Bennett, the age level of record purchasers kept plummeting until 1958, when teenagers were buying 70 per cent of all records. Simultaneously the world of popular music was inundated by a wild new sound called rock and roll, a thundering mixture of country-western music with Negro rhythm and blues. The performers who introduced the new sound *(pages 142-147)* struck most adults as being callow, pimply faced boys with ducktail haircuts and untrained voices, emitting mindless and frequently repulsive grunts. The rhythm of rock seemed overpowering and monotonous, the volume deafening and the movements made by performers scandalous. Even more scandalous were some of the lyrics: "Make me feel real loose, Like a long-necked goose. Oh, Baby, that's-a what I like." In fact, the very term "rock and roll," coined by New York disc jockey Alan Freed, was inspired by a raunchy old blues lyric, "My baby rocks me with a steady roll." Yet the new genre was clearly irresistible to the teen-age girls who now dominated the music market; they made national idols (and overnight millionaires) of adolescent guitar-thumpers and bought rock records in quantities beyond the wildest pop dreams of Dinah Shore and even Frank Sinatra. The genteel singers on TV's traditional pop showcase *Your Hit Parade* sounded like fools when they tried to warble "You Ain't Nothin' But a Hound Dog," and by mid-1957 the program went off the air, drowned by the teen-age tidal wave of rock and roll.

Pop star Rosemary Clooney displays the goodies she will give to the man who accepts her hit-song invitation to "Come On-a My House."

Many first ladies of popular music in the '50s came up
via the nightclub circuit, where their acts were honed for the expense-account
crowds of businessmen on the town. Five of
these big stars are shown below, each with the name of her biggest pop hit.

PATTI PAGE
Tennessee Waltz

JO STAFFORD
Shrimp Boats

TERESA BREWER
Music! Music! Music!

KAY STARR
Wheel of Fortune

PEGGY LEE
Fever

Unlike the much simpler paper record covers of the '40s, LP albums were embellished with arty photographs and the latest in graphic fads.

Though the adult music popular in the first half of the '50s all came under the single artistic heading of "mood," the performers who got rich by recording that mood represented a whole spectrum of styles and tastes. The unctuous pianist Liberace made up to one million dollars a year by tinkling his way to the hearts of middle-aged ladies who doted on his brand of candlelit schmaltz; a bearded orchestra leader named Mitch Miller sold 1.75 million albums within 15 months by persuading listeners alone in their homes to sing along with his folksy music. One of the most successful of the recording artists was lithe, handsome Harry Belafonte, who scored for RCA with an album called "Calypso," the first LP to sell a million copies. From then through 1960, employing a combination of calypso and folk style spiced with a heaping measure of sex appeal, Belafonte earned a cool $750,000 per year.

A Swinging Prophet

The man who turned rock and roll into a national teenage religion was a 21-year-old Memphis truck driver named Elvis Presley. And he did it, of all places, on the Dorsey brothers' TV show, one of the bastions of four-sided pop music. The moment Elvis stepped to the mike and set his electric guitar to bellowing with a series of full-armed whacks, it was obvious that he was different. His voice shouted and trembled as though it, too, were electrified; and his way of moving was nothing short of orgiastic. So freely did Elvis bump, grind and shimmy his way through the show that Ed Sullivan pronounced him "unfit for a family audience."

The young girls in virtually every American family pronounced otherwise. Presley's first LP record *(right)* leaped to the top of *Billboard* magazine's weekly ratings; his singles ("Heartbreak Hotel," "Don't Be Cruel" and "Love Me Tender") each sold over a million copies. Finally, in late 1956, Ed Sullivan took a large bite of crow and hired Elvis for three appearances at an unprecedented $50,000, while still insisting that Presley be permitted on camera only from the waist up.

Although Elvis turned rock into an opiate for teenagers, he did not invent the form—a blending of the music of white back-country balladeers with Negro rhythm-and-blues that had been evolving gradually as social strictures loosened and each became more aware of the other. Then in 1954 a Negro group, the Chords, hit it big when they wrote "Sh-Boom," and in 1955 Bill Haley and his all-white Comets scored with "Rock Around the Clock." But somehow Haley, et al., lacked the sex appeal to capture the youth market.

Enter, with a crash, Elvis Presley, followed by imitators *(pages 146-147)* who wiggled, wailed and cashed in handsomely but never truly threatened the prophet himself. By 1960 Elvis alone had sold $120 million worth of records, sheet music, movie tickets and merchandise; the T-shirt and tight dungarees he had worn as a poor kid in Memphis had given way to $10,000 gold lamé suits; and the truck he had driven for a living had been replaced by a fleet of gleaming pastel Cadillacs.

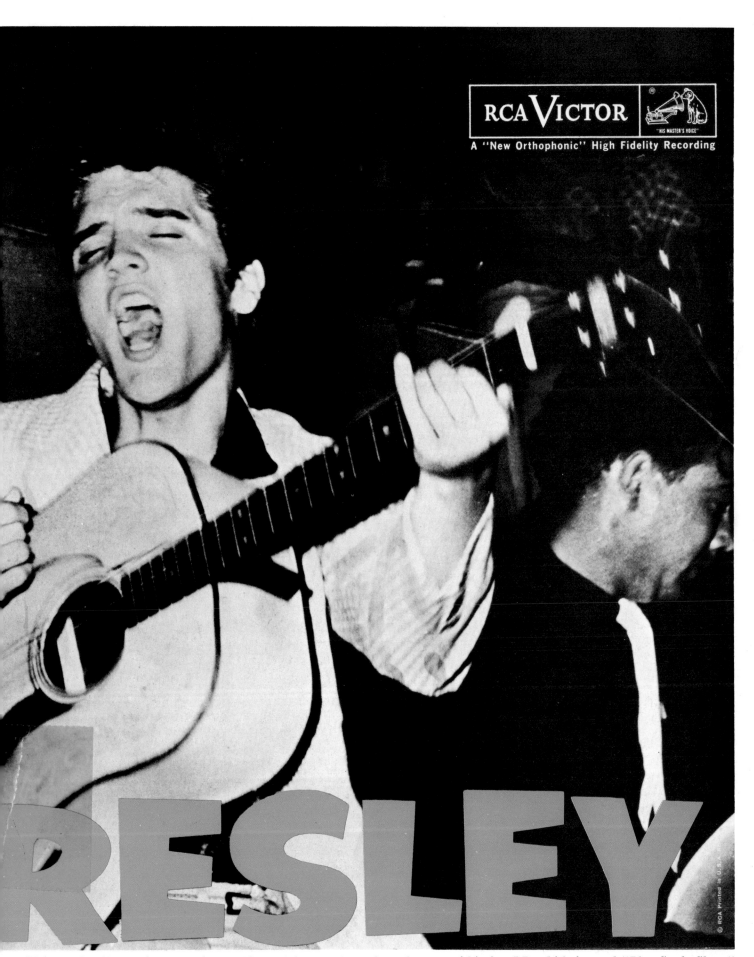

RCA VICTOR

A "New Orthophonic" High Fidelity Recording

PRESLEY

Elvis manhandles a microphone in Las Vegas (left) and shouts from the cover of his first LP, which featured "Blue Suede Shoes."

Elvis drives fans wild during a 1956 show, but privately he giggled at his ability to elicit shrieks of delight just by pointing a finger.

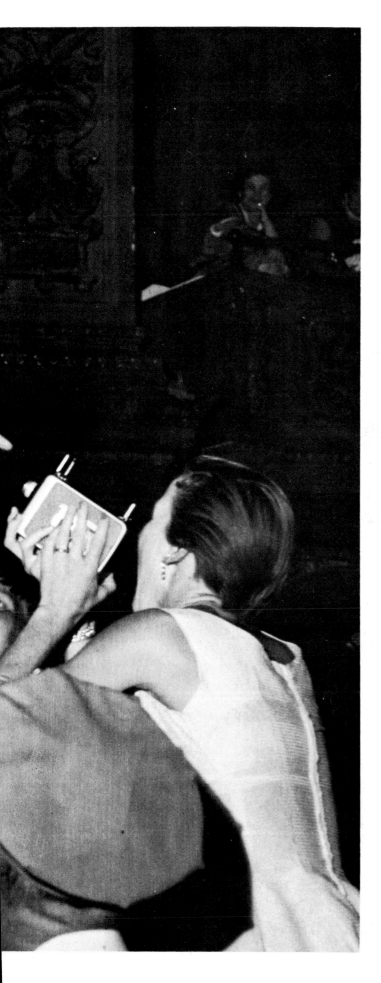

Beneath all the stage wriggling, the lustful tough-guy looks and the Cadillacs, Elvis was really a nice, gentle country boy who neither smoked nor drank. Careful interviewers found to their surprise that he always said his prayers before bed, loved and obeyed his parents, and addressed all adults as "Sir" or "Ma'am." ("The only trouble I have falling asleep is when I think of my success, sir," he told one reporter.) But this was not the Elvis most of the world saw. And his visceral public style drew broadsides of wrath from scores of newspaper columnists, as the excerpts below indicate.

It isn't enough to say that Elvis is kind to his parents. That still isn't a free ticket to behave like a sex maniac in public before millions of impressionable kids. According to a scholarly friend of mine, Jackie Gleason, we'll survive Elvis. "He can't last," said Gleason. "I tell you flatly—he can't last."

EDDIE CONDON, *NEW YORK JOURNAL-AMERICAN*, 1956

Presley and his voodoo of frustration and defiance have become symbols in our country, and we are sorry to come upon Ed Sullivan in the role of promoter. Your Catholic viewers, Mr. Sullivan, are angry; and you cannot compensate for a moral injury, not even by sticking "The Little Gaelic Singers of County Derry" on the same bill with Elvis Presley.

THE REVEREND WILLIAM J. SHANNON, *CATHOLIC SUN*, 1956

On the Sullivan program Presley injected movements of the tongue and indulged in wordless singing that were singularly distasteful. When Presley executes his bumps and grinds, it must be remembered by the Columbia Broadcasting System that even the 12-year-old's curiosity may be overstimulated.

JACK GOULD, *THE NEW YORK TIMES*, 1956

Rock and roll stars were almost all young men, belting
out their famous hits to the most avid rock fans—young girls. Singers like
the Everly Brothers were excellent musicians, but the likes
of Fabian, who could scarcely hold a note, were idolized as typical teens.

FABIAN
Turn Me Loose

LITTLE ANTHONY
Tears on My Pillow

FRANKIE AVALON
Venus

BOBBY DARIN
Mack the Knife

EVERLY BROTHERS
All I Have To Do Is Dream

YD PRICE
sonality

RICKY NELSON
Poor Little Fool

At his telecast 29th birthday party Clark greets Sal Mineo. Others include, at far left, rock singers Darin, Avalon and Boone.

Entrepreneur of Bedlam

Along with creating prosperous heroes from a flock of young singers, rock spawned the inevitable entrepreneurs who found ways to make hefty middleman's profits from the new sound. The most visible of these middlemen were the disc jockeys, and their undisputed king was a well-scrubbed square in his mid-twenties named Dick Clark, master of ceremonies for an afternoon TV show called *American Bandstand.*

Playing to the astounding total of 20 million regular weekday viewers, Clark paraded a stream of top rock stars before his cameras. But these celebrities rarely sang live on the show; rather, with a record of one of their hits going full blast, they moved their lips in synchronization with the sound. This technique was absolutely necessary for many of the unschooled rock singers. Once, when Clark asked Fabian to sing live a few bars from "Mary Had a Little Lamb," Fabian had to rehearse dozens of times.

While presiding over the parade of singers, Clark established his own weekly ratings of hits that became a national pecking order for rock stars. And he threw open the floor of his sprawling TV studio to young fans so that they could come on and dance while the music thundered. This odd entertainment earned Clark some $500,000 a year, 50,000 fan letters a week and the fawning attention of would-be rock singers, whom he could make or break at will. Connie Francis, Fabian and Bobby Darin, to name just three, owed their success to Clark's patronage. So influential did Clark become that one record-company salesman remarked that if Clark played a record "once a day for a week on his show, we could count on a sale in the stores of at least two hundred and fifty thousand."

This influence also earned Clark an investigation from the House of Representatives to see whether his rating of records and hopeful singers represented impartial judgments of merit. The probe cleared Clark of bribe-taking but did establish that the *Bandstand* emcee's financial interests were not harmed by the fact that he owned a record-pressing plant, a music publishing company, and a talent management firm.

DICK CLARK, *BANDSTAND* EMCEE

Through all the hubbub, Clark remained the bland, short-haired square whose mission was to champion the cause of rock and roll: "What I'm trying to defend," he once wrote, "is my right and your right to go to a church of our choice, or buy the record of our choice." Typical of his boostership and sweetness-and-light approach was the system he devised for rating new releases; though his scale ran from zero to 100, he never rated a tune below 35 or over 98, "on the theory that no record is completely good or completely bad."

Teen-age fans adored this square peg who fitted so smoothly into their world. They lined up in regiments to get into his show so that they could rock and roll before his cameras—a fling performed so appealingly by some that they became bona fide celebrities in their own right. Most famous of the fans-turned-dancers was a winsome little blonde named Justine Corelli, who received hundreds of fan letters each week. Her sometime partner, Kenny Rossi, a 14-year-old "regular" in 1958, had 301 fan clubs.

One elderly viewer wrote Clark: "Please, Dick, as a special favor to an old farm woman, I would like to see Tony in another spotlight dance. Please do this, as Tony reminds me of someone I loved long, long ago and lost by death." So real did the electronic life of *Bandstand* become to viewers and participants that when a reporter asked dancing regular Mary Ann Cuff her plans for the future, she replied, "We *Bandstand* kids have a crazy dream. It's a baby idea. Maybe I better not say." "Oh, tell her," someone urged. "Well," Mary Ann confided, "What it is we all want is to get married and live on the same street in new houses. We'll call it Bandstand Ave."

Rock and roll singers lip-synch a hit to the loud blare of a record.

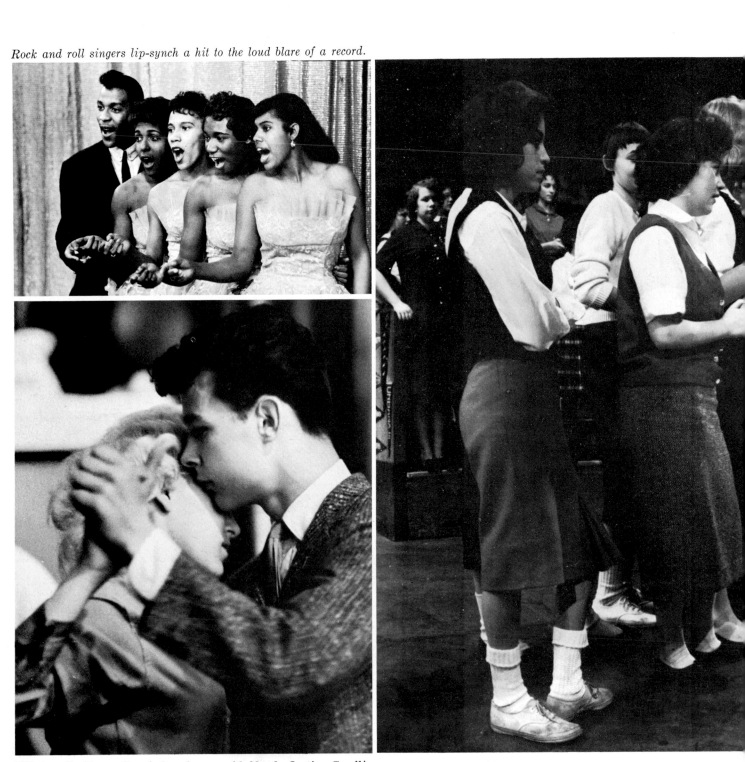

TV favorite Kenny Rossi slow-dances with blonde Justine Corelli.

As rock and roll stars mouthed their hit records, kids who flocked

to the "American Bandstand" show expertly performed the latest dance crazes such as

the Hand Jive or the Bop. They even invented three

dances: the Stroll, the Circle and a modified cha-cha they called the Chalypso.

A couple does the Slop, as 150 others on the show clap to the rhythm. To such regulars, other visiting fans were "The Amateurs."

The Big Sellers

The chart shown here of the 10 top records
for each year traces the triumph of rock and roll over pop.
But the old style did not die out completely:
The No. 1 record for 1957 was Debbie Reynolds' "Tammy."

1950

1 GOODNIGHT IRENE
The Weavers and Gordon Jenkins
2 IT ISN'T FAIR—Sammy Kaye
3 THIRD MAN THEME—Anton Karas
4 MULE TRAIN—Frankie Laine
5 MONA LISA—Nat "King" Cole
6 MUSIC! MUSIC! MUSIC!—Teresa Brewer
7 I WANNA BE LOVED—Andrews Sisters
8 IF I KNEW YOU WERE COMIN'
I'D'VE BAKED A CAKE—Eileen Barton
9 I CAN DREAM CAN'T I—Andrews Sisters
10 THAT LUCKY OLD SUN—Frankie Laine

1951

1 TENNESSEE WALTZ—Patti Page
2 HOW HIGH THE MOON
Les Paul and Mary Ford
3 TOO YOUNG—Nat "King" Cole
4 BE MY LOVE—Mario Lanza
5 BECAUSE OF YOU—Tony Bennett
6 ON TOP OF OLD SMOKY
The Weavers and Gordon Jenkins
7 IF—Perry Como
8 SIN—Eddy Howard
9 COME ON-A MY HOUSE—Rosemary Clooney
10 MOCKIN' BIRD HILL—Patti Page

1954

1 LITTLE THINGS MEAN A LOT
Kitty Kallen
2 HEY THERE—Rosemary Clooney
3 WANTED—Perry Como
4 YOUNG AT HEART—Frank Sinatra
5 SH-BOOM—The Crew Cuts
6 THREE COINS IN THE FOUNTAIN
The Four Aces
7 LITTLE SHOEMAKER—The Gaylords
8 OH! MY PA-PA—Eddie Fisher
9 SECRET LOVE—Doris Day
10 HAPPY WANDERER—Frank Weir

1957

1 TAMMY—Debbie Reynolds
2 LOVE LETTERS IN THE SAND
Pat Boone
3 IT'S NOT FOR ME TO SAY
Johnny Mathis
4 YOUNG LOVE—Tab Hunter
5 CHANCES ARE—Johnny Mathis
6 LITTLE DARLIN'—The Diamonds
7 BYE BYE LOVE—The Everly Brothers
8 ALL SHOOK UP—Elvis Presley
9 SO RARE—Jimmy Dorsey
10 ROUND AND ROUND—Perry Como

1952

1 CRY—Johnnie Ray
2 BLUE TANGO
Leroy Anderson
3 ANY TIME—Eddie Fisher
4 DELICADO—Percy Faith
5 KISS OF FIRE—Georgia Gibbs
6 WHEEL OF FORTUNE—Kay Starr
7 TELL ME WHY—The Four Aces
8 I'M YOURS—Don Cornell
9 HERE IN MY HEART—Al Martino
10 AUF WIEDERSEH'N, SWEETHEART
Vera Lynn

1955

1 ROCK AROUND THE CLOCK
Bill Haley and the Comets
2 BALLAD OF DAVY CROCKETT—Bill Hayes
3 CHERRY PINK AND
APPLE BLOSSOM WHITE—Perez Prado
4 MELODY OF LOVE—Billy Vaughn
5 YELLOW ROSE OF TEXAS—Mitch Miller
6 AIN'T THAT A SHAME—Pat Boone
7 SINCERELY—The McGuire Sisters
8 UNCHAINED MELODY—Les Baxter
9 CRAZY OTTO RAG—Crazy Otto
10 MISTER SANDMAN—The Chordettes

1958

1 VOLARE (NEL BLU, DIPINTO DI BLU)
Domenico Modugno
2 IT'S ALL IN THE GAME—Tommy Edwards
3 PATRICIA—Perez Prado
4 ALL I HAVE TO DO IS DREAM
The Everly Brothers
5 BIRD DOG—The Everly Brothers
6 LITTLE STAR—The Elegants
7 WITCH DOCTOR—David Seville
8 TWILIGHT TIME—The Platters
9 TEQUILA—The Champs
10 AT THE HOP—Danny and The Juniors

1953

1 SONG FROM THE MOULIN ROUGE
Percy Faith
2 TILL I WALTZ AGAIN WITH YOU
Teresa Brewer
3 APRIL IN PORTUGAL—Lee Baxter
4 VAYA CON DIOS—Les Paul and Mary Ford
5 I'M WALKING BEHIND YOU—Eddie Fisher
6 I BELIEVE—Frankie Laine
7 YOU YOU YOU—The Ames Brothers
8 DOGGIE IN THE WINDOW—Patti Page
9 WHY DON'T YOU BELIEVE ME—Joni James
10 PRETEND—Nat "King" Cole

1956

1 DON'T BE CRUEL—Elvis Presley
2 GREAT PRETENDER—The Platters
3 MY PRAYER—The Platters
4 WAYWARD WIND—Gogi Grant
5 WHATEVER WILL BE, WILL BE
Doris Day
6 HEARTBREAK HOTEL—Elvis Presley
7 LISBON ANTIGUA—Nelson Riddle
8 CANADIAN SUNSET—Hugo Winterhalter
9 MOONGLOW and THEME
FROM "PICNIC"—Morris Stoloff
10 HONKY TONK—Bill Doggett

1959

1 MACK THE KNIFE—Bobby Darin
2 BATTLE OF NEW ORLEANS
Johnny Horton
3 VENUS—Frankie Avalon
4 LONELY BOY—Paul Anka
5 THERE GOES MY BABY—The Drifters
6 PERSONALITY—Lloyd Price
7 THREE BELLS—The Browns
8 PUT YOUR HEAD ON MY SHOULDER
Paul Anka
9 SLEEP WALK—Santo and Johnny
10 COME SOFTLY TO ME—The Fleetwoods

One of the few singers to survive the transition from pop to rock, Pat Boone smiles through a collar of gold records (million-plus sellers).

Suburbia

Levittown, New York, once a potato farm, had 17,447 houses by 1951.

The Battle of Babyville

The Moving Van is a symbol of more than our restlessness; it is the most conclusive possible evidence of our progress.   LOUIS KRONENBERGER, *COMPANY MANNERS,* 1951

Some were rising executives; others only thought they were or pretended to be. Some were lawyers, dentists, steamfitters, teachers, stockbrokers, butchers, cops. In the '50s they moved by the millions to the suburbs, and the suburbs spread like patches of fungus to make room for them. There were houses for nearly everybody (1.396 million brand-new ones in 1950 alone), from eight-bedroom mansions on two-acre plots of ground ($62,000 in Greenwich, Connecticut) to little look-alike $6,000 boxes five feet apart in Daly City, California. And there were babies—so many that babyville became a synonym for suburbia.

Most of the new suburbanites said they had left the city in search of clean air, space, green stuff to look at and good schools. They usually got those things, but many had a more elusive goal that they did not discuss as freely: higher social status. Young husbands hoped for influential neighbors who might help them in their careers. Wives dreamed of entertainment in more sophisticated homes than they had known. To an extent these hopes came true. Status is self-conferrable. Cheerfully the new suburbs conferred it on themselves.

There were disadvantages. The men had weary commutes to work, either by faltering railroads (in 1955 nearly 40 per cent of all New York, New Haven and Hartford trains were at least five minutes late) or crowded highways. They were faced with unaccustomed burdens such as lawnmowing. Taxes rose steeply to support the schools that were needed. Children could no longer be left with Grandma; she was usually out of reach, so when parents went out in the evenings, they had to employ a babysitter at 75 cents an hour.

The typical new suburb *(pages 154-155)* started from scratch on vacant land sold to subdividers, and its inhabitants hardly knew how to begin. Carefully they tended their grounds to win neighbors' approval and held backyard barbecues to cement chance acquaintanceships. They set up branches of national institutions —the Girl Scouts, the Little League, the P.T.A. and Cub Scouts—and sent their children to music and dancing classes. Cocktail parties grew into cocktail circuits and, though they were often derided, to be invited was a mark of social acceptance. By the decade's close many a new suburb had built a convincing replica of Scarsdale —and already a few restless citizens were buying camping equipment to escape into the wilderness.

"*I want to talk about something besides kids and illness!*"

DRAWING BY CLAUDE. COPR. © 1956 THE NEW YORKER MAGAZINE, INC.

Commuters	1950	1960
COMMUTER RAILROADS	46	30
RAIL COMMUTER PASSENGER RIDES *millions*	277	203
NEW YORK CITY AUTO COMMUTERS *thousands*	640 *est.*	866

Railroads cut back on their service. More and more commuters turned to highway transportation, as shown above in New York City.

This New York Central train on a January 1958 evening has seats for all. Many commuter trains had not, and passengers had to stand.

The 5:57 discharges commuters in Park Forest, Illinois. As commuter lines and facilities decreased, a national transit crisis loomed.

"*My husband is the exact size of our picture window.*"

DRAWING BY PETER WYMA

Housing	1950	1960
U.S. HOMEOWNERS *millions*	23.6	32.8
NEW HOUSING UNITS STARTED *millions*	1.4	1.3
LAWN AND PORCH FURNITURE SALES *millions of dollars*	53.6	145.2

By 1960, with the peak postwar housing shortages already met, housing starts declined, but the sales of accessories, such as lawn and porch furniture, soared.

This development house was built in Sacramento at the peak of the boom. Lawn decorations like the flamingo above were standard items.

On a typically sunny day in Santa Barbara, California, the entire family gathers in the backyard for the ritual Sunday afternoon barbecue.

"*Remember, Herbert, medium-burnt, not well-burnt.*"

DRAWING BY HENRY BOLTINOFF

The Barbeque	1950	1960
HOT DOG PRODUCTION *millions lbs.—est.*	750	1050
POTATO CHIP PRODUCTION *millions lbs.—est.*	320	532

The relatively minor increase in hot dog production reflected a turn to fancier, more substantial fare like hamburgers, steak, chicken, shish kebab and spare ribs.

DRAWING BY KAUFMAN, MC CALL'S

Home Chores	1950	1960
POWER MOWERS SOLD *millions*	1.0	3.8
FLOOR POLISHERS SOLD *millions*	0.24	1.0
AUTOMATIC WASHING MACHINES SOLD *millions*	1.7	2.6

With help expensive and hard to find, suburbanites launched a campaign of do-it-yourself maintenance.

A homeowner in Baton Rouge cuts his lawn with a rotary mower. Rotaries, able to go most anywhere, became the most popular design.

The eight members of a family in Port Washington, New York, wash their station wagon. In their expert hands, the job took seven minutes.

A father herds his daughter and her fellow Brownies—plus one stray kid brother—to their regular Saturday ice-skating lesson.

"Am I glad to see you!!!"

© SATURDAY EVENING POST 1954

Children	1950	1960
CHILDREN 5-14 *millions*	24.3	35.5
LITTLE LEAGUES	776.0	5,700.0
GIRL SCOUTS AND BROWNIES *millions*	1.8	4.0
BICYCLE PRODUCTION *domestic and imported, millions*	2.0	3.8

Suburbia's raison d'être was good schools, community life and healthy surroundings. It all added up to kids.

Two den mothers join their Cub Scouts in the pledge of allegiance.

"Oh, Walt, just look at her! Doesn't
the ten-dollars-a-lesson seem insignificant now?"

Higher Horizons	1950	1960
ENCYCLOPEDIA SALES *millions of dollars*	72	300
MUSICAL INSTRUMENT SALES *millions of dollars*	86	149
JUVENILE BOOK SALES *millions of dollars*	32 *est.*	88

*Pushed by ambitious parents, the sales of encyclopedias
—and all sorts of other cultural enrichments—boomed.*

Youngsters line up in a Columbus, Indiana, dancing class. In suburbia, parents were expected to give children the "advantages."

A hostess in Little Rock, Arkansas, charms guests with her own canapés. Some daring housewives even assayed rattlesnake meat.

"Oh, oh, they've got the dictionary out. It's going to be one of THOSE evenings!"

The Cocktail Party	1950	1960
GIN PRODUCTION *millions of tax gallons— domestic and imported*	6	19
VODKA PRODUCTION *millions of tax gallons— domestic*	0.1 *est.*	9
ASPIRIN SALES *millions of pounds*	12	18

In communities where people were new, nothing broke the ice quicker than liquor. Suburbia was known for its consumption of alcoholic beverages.

A friendly host makes the classic gesture of passing a drink to an eager hand at a party in his home in Farmington, Michigan.

"*Been a great bowling season, dear. Both the kids O.K.?*"
STAR WEEKLY

HARRY JONES

Recreation

	1950	1960
NATIONAL FOREST CAMPERS *millions*	1.5	6.6
BOWLING LANES *thousands*	52.5	108.0
OUTBOARD MOTORS IN USE *millions*	2.8	5.8

Suburbia was not only a new place to live, it was a new way to live, with more active sports, more simple fun.

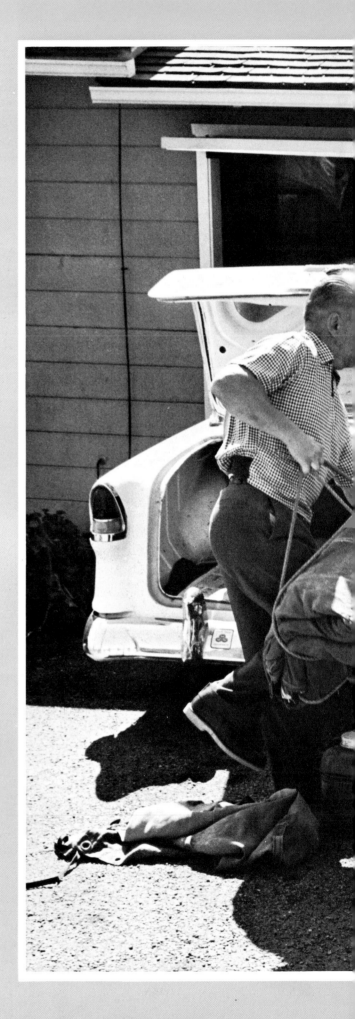

A family in Santa Barbara, California, packs for a camp-out. During the decade the number of recreation seekers more than doubled.

Art lovers gather on the ramp of Manhattan's Guggenheim Museum, which opened in 1959.

Culture

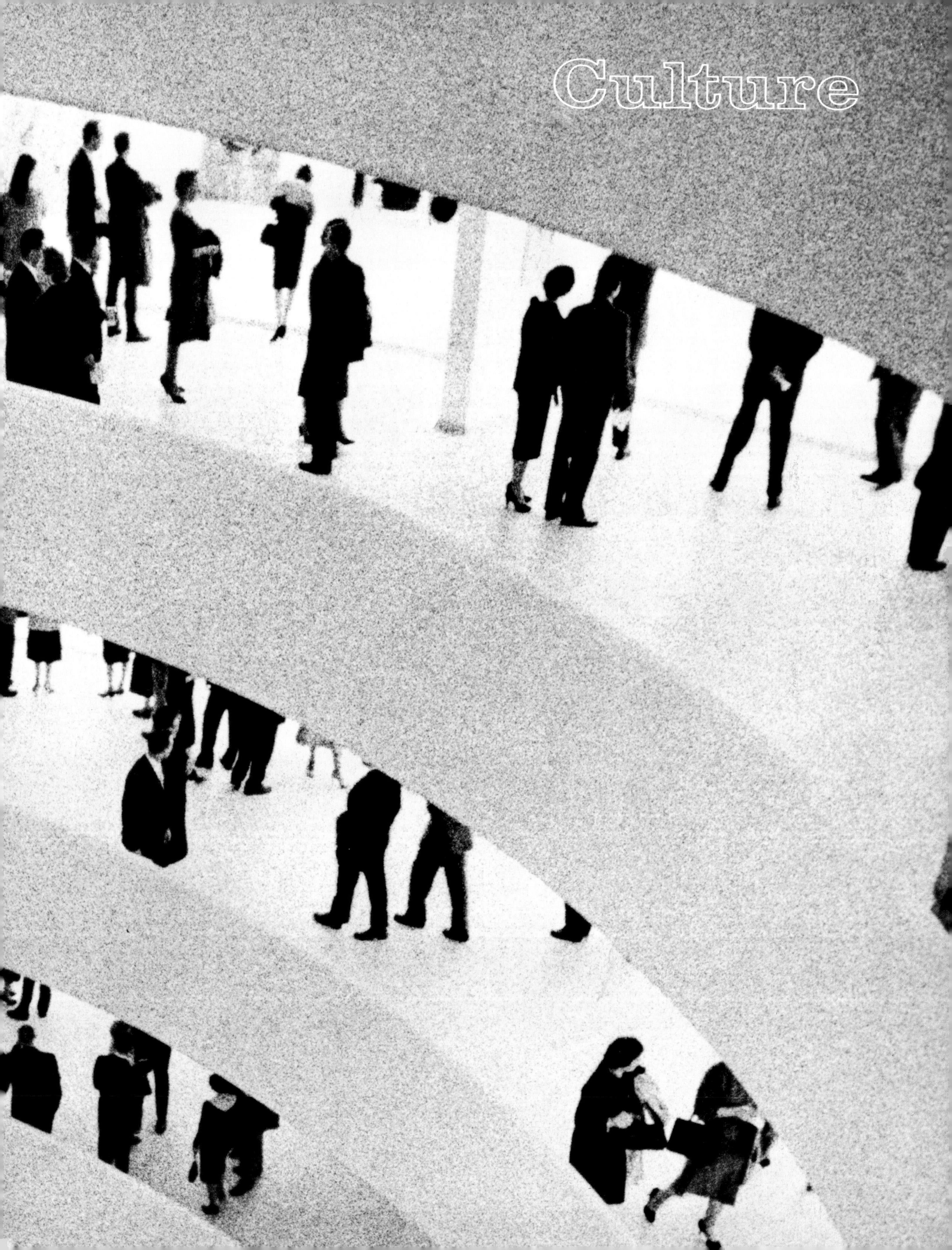

The Cultural Muddle

There seems to be a Gresham's Law in cultural as well as monetary circulation: bad stuff drives out the good, since it is more easily understood and enjoyed.

DWIGHT MACDONALD IN *DIOGENES*, 1953

The prevailing mood is one of pessimism; in literary and intellectual circles there is much more talk of decadence than of renaissance. CECIL HEMLEY IN *COMMONWEAL*, 1954

Most critics, especially the highbrow kind *(above)*, deplored the mass culture of the '50s. And there was plenty to deplore. The preponderance of popular fare —Hollywood spectaculars, "horror" comics, hammering rock-and-roll music—had only one redeeming virtue: transience. Television was everyone's whipping boy; and in contemplating its fare, even middlebrow columnist Harriet Van Horne was crying cultural doom: "Our people are becoming less literate by the minute.... As old habits decline, such as reading books and thinking thoughts, TV will absorb their time. By the 21st Century our people doubtless will be squint-eyed, hunchbacked and fond of the dark."

There were real cultural dangers, no doubt of it. In this age of economic boom and mass media, culture, like toothpaste, was produced and consumed at a fearful rate; and this relentless pressure did tend to lower the quality of the product. Yet the situation was not so dismal as the pessimists claimed. For one thing, the much-abused media seemed quite responsible at times. In 1956, the National Broadcasting Company paid out $500,000 to present the premier of Laurence Olivier's film version of Shakespeare's *Richard III*. Fifty million people tuned in, and about half of them stayed on through its entire three hours. *Life* magazine in 1952 regaled—or challenged—its several million readers by devoting a whole issue to the publication of Ernest Hemingway's new novel, *The Old Man and the Sea*.

There were other oases in the cultural wasteland. In painting, a group of innovators led by Jackson Pollock moved the capital of the art world from Paris to New York. Egghead humor, as purveyed by sharp-tongued satirists such as Mort Sahl, graduated from small clubs to big audiences on network variety shows. Paperback publishers propagated millions of copies of standard classics at prices low enough ($0.25 to $1.35) to attract cultural window-shoppers. Classical music was riding a spectacular wave of national interest. In mid-decade the country boasted some 200 symphony orchestras, up 80 per cent since 1940, and 2,500 towns offered concert series, an increase of 150 per cent in the same period. Music, in fact, went a long way toward proving that America's cultural oases might yet become bigger than the wasteland itself: in 1955 some 35 million people went to classical music performances—more than twice the year's attendance at major league baseball games.

An earnest art lover peers quizzically at a welded wire statue by Kahlil Gibran, one of 1,500 works in a Madison Square Garden show.

Standing on a 17-foot canvas in his studio barn in the village of Springs, Long Island, Pollock drips and splatters enamel paint.

Jack the Dripper

In the mid-'40s, a handful of avant-garde art critics were caught up by the vast abstract canvases of a nonconformist named Jackson Pollock. The best known of the spontaneous "action" painters, Pollock dribbled paint on the canvas with a stick (left) or poured it directly from a can. From this his detractors (including "Time" magazine) dubbed him "Jack the Dripper" and described his art as "an explosion in a shingle mill." To those who vainly searched his work for a hidden message, Pollock had a word of advice: "It's just like a bed of flowers. You don't have to tear your hair out over what it means." By 1956 Pollock had won many converts, but in August of that year he lost his life in an automobile accident. Subsequently many of the same critics who made sport of him hailed him as "one of the greatest artists of our time." The final confirmation of his status came in 1960 —when a Jackson Pollock sold for $100,000.

Jon Whitcomb's illustration for the "Ladies' Home Journal" is as simple as its breathless caption: "I'm so happy I could die."

An impressionistic Coca-Cola ad is divided into panels by foreground trees; the background is in the new dappled-brush technique.

Commercial Art Goes Arty

Like the fine arts, commercial art in the '50s underwent a major
revolt against tradition. Slick, photographlike illustrations were "out." The "in" picture
was more sophisticated in design, more cosmopolitan
in subject matter (above). Said commercial artist Austin Briggs: "Let's remind
ourselves that last year's fresh idea is today's cliché."

Instant Masterpieces

In 1952 the Palmer Paint Company of Detroit put out kits for
amateur painters with color-coded canvases ranging from the sublime (below) to the
ridiculous, like the fan club portraits of Jimmy Durante (opposite).
Twelve million aspiring artists bought these kits, including one who was awarded third
prize at a bona fide San Francisco art show by unsuspecting judges.

A by-the-numbers rendering of "The Last Supper" sold for $11.50. Included in the price was a "beautiful antique gold frame."

On and Off the Rialto

Broadway took few risks during the '50s, banking heavily on big musicals of the kind that had set attendance records in the '40s. Typical of these was Meredith Willson's *The Music Man,* a corny family show about a con artist who tries to dupe a little Iowa town in 1912—but ends up as lovable as everyone else on the stage. Rodgers and Hammerstein, naturally, remained at the top of the field, scoring in 1951 with *The King and I,* in 1958 with *Flower Drum Song* and a year later with *Sound of Music.*

The biggest single hit of the decade was Lerner and Loewe's *My Fair Lady,* a musical adaptation of George Bernard Shaw's *Pygmalion.* Set in Edwardian England, the plot revolved around the attempt of Henry Higgins, a professor of phonetics (Rex Harrison), to teach Eliza Doolittle, a cockney girl (Julie Andrews), how to speak like a lady. Higgins succeeded, but Harrison very nearly flopped before the first curtain went up. Below he describes the struggles of composer Frederick Loewe and lyricist Alan Jay Lerner to convert him from a nonsinging dra-

matic actor into a musical comedy performer—a feat as formidable as the transformation of Eliza into a lady.

Two other successful variations on the Broadway theme were *Bye, Bye Birdie,* which spoofed a rock and roll singer resembling Elvis Presley, and *West Side Story.* Both shows modeled their heroes on America's newly rebellious youth, but *Birdie* was pure froth, while *West Side Story* was a powerful retelling of the tragic tale of *Romeo and Juliet* in terms of rival teen-age slum gangs.

The one new stage development of the decade was the growth of off-Broadway productions. The $250,000-plus cost of putting on a Broadway show and scalper prices up to $50 for orchestra seats triggered a migration downtown to low-cost houses in Greenwich Village. In 1954 *The Three-Penny Opera* opened there with an eyedropper budget of $9,000 and tickets scaled down as low as $1.75. Its dramatic excellence spurred an enormously successful rush of hole-in-the-wall productions, and, by 1956, off-Broadway was offering 68 shows to adventurous theatergoers.

Only once before had I ever sung on stage, and my reception indicated to me that I should never do a musical again. I spent an afternoon with Lerner and Loewe round a piano singing Gilbert and Sullivan, and so as to hide any embarrassment I might have, they sang along with me. If I remember correctly, it was dismal.

Anyway, once given all of my songs, it was suggested diplomatically that I go and have my voice—"placed" I think is the term. The first teacher I went to tried to train me in bel canto singing, which, of course, was ri-

diculous. After six lessons I chucked it, and when Lerner and Loewe returned to London I hadn't learned a thing. They then found me an instructor who was a tremendous believer in the use of the same mechanical methods for the spoken and sung word. Once again I began to sound like my natural, horrible self. I confess that if the conductor had not watched me constantly I'd have been lost. It's miraculous the way that he follows me, since, as I understand it, I'm supposed to be following him. As Higgins says, I am at best really just an ordinary man.

NEW YORK HERALD TRIBUNE, MAY 13, 1956

In the musical, "My Fair Lady," Rex Harrison teaches Julie Andrews to say her "h's": "In Hartford, Hereford and Hampshire. . . ."

The very model of a square but happy musician, Robert Preston directs a small-fry Iowa band in the 1957 hit "The Music Man."

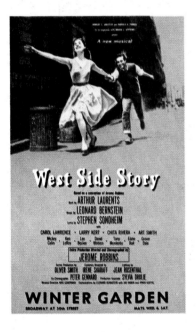

In "Bye, Bye Birdie," rock-and-roll star Conrad Birdie sings to a bevy of ecstatic teenagers.

In "West Side Story," a street-gang musical of "Romeo and Juliet," hoods with switchblades reenact the duel between Romeo and Tybalt.

The Healthiest Mummy

"The Threepenny Opera,"
off-Broadway's big hit of the '50s, opened in
Greenwich Village September 20, 1955,
and at decade's end was still going strong after 2,000
performances. The show, a modern
version of John Gay's 18th Century "The Beggar's
Opera," had had a successful run in
Berlin in 1928 but flopped in New York in 1933.
Critics denounced it as "a mummy
grinning upon a dunghill"; 22 years later they
cheerfully reversed that verdict: ". . . superb. It vividly
expresses the casual, squalid, hugger-
mugger of the fable." Recordings of the show's top
tune, "Mack the Knife," sold over
10 million copies—a total surpassed only by
"White Christmas."

Mack the Knife, sadistic and sexy leader of Soho's underworld, makes a mad pass at Jennie, a tawdry barmaid, as a beggar looks on.

Blood and Gutters

Although some book publishers gloomily predicted at the beginning of the '50s that TV would blow them right out of business, they were astonished to find, at decade's end, that they had sold 53 per cent more books than in the previous 10 years. And the chairman of the board of Simon & Schuster actually thanked TV for this boom: people stayed home to watch their favorite shows, he explained, and when the show was over, it was "too late to go out and too early to go to bed." So they read books.

To meet this new demand, publishers began producing huge stocks of cheap paperbacks, using machinery adapted from the magazine industry to print 12,000 soft-cover volumes an hour. Some were priced as low as 25 cents and by 1958, the astonishing total of 350 million books were sold in one year. Atop this wave, raking in royalties of as much as $56,000 a year, were sensationalists like Grace Metalious, author of *Peyton Place*, a novel about life in a New England Gomorrah *(page 195)*, and a tough-talking Brooklyn writer named Frank Morrison (Mickey) Spillane *(right)*. Spillane's detective hero Mike Hammer left in his wake after six books more than 45 corpses and countless beautiful, ravaged babes. Mystery fans devoured 27 million copies of Spillane's alleged trash, reveling in passages like the one below from *Kiss Me, Deadly*. Samples of other leading fiction sellers appear on the following pages.

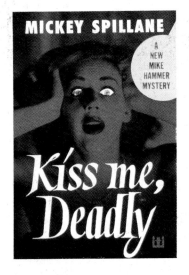

I *stepped across the body and picked up the phone. I called headquarters and tried to get Pat. He was still out. I had the call transferred to another department and the man I wanted said hello. I asked him for the identification on a dead blonde and he told me to wait.*

A minute later he picked up the phone.

"*Think I got it. Death by drowning. Age, about . . .*"

"*Skip the details. Just the name.*"

"*Sure. Lily Carver. Prints just came in from Washington. She had 'em taken while she worked at a war plant.*" *I said thanks, held the button down on the phone, let it go and when I heard the dial tone started working on my home number.*

She said, "*Don't bother, Mike. I'm right here.*"

And she was. Beautiful Lily with hair as white as snow. Her mouth a scarlet curve that smiled. Differently, now, but still smiling. Her body a tight bundle of lush curves that swelled and moved under a light white terrycloth robe. Lovely Lily who brought the sharpness of an alcohol bath in with her so that it wet her robe until there was nothing there, no hill or valley, no shadow that didn't come out.

Gorgeous Lily with my .45 in her hand from where she had found it on the dresser.

"*You forgot about me, Mike.*"

"*I almost did, didn't I.*"

There was cold hate coming into her eyes now. Hate that grew as she looked again at the one eye in the body beside the table. "*You shouldn't have done that, Mike.*"

"*No?*"

"*He was the only one who knew about me.*" *The smile left her mouth.* "*I loved him. He knew about me and didn't care. I loved him, you crumb you!*"

Ruggedly attired in a T-shirt, mystery-writer Mickey Spillane chats about success in his hand-built bungalow in Newburgh, New York.

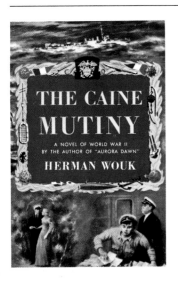

The helmsman called, "Steadying up on 220, sir."

"WHAT?" yelled Queeg. He dived into the pilot-house. "Who gave you the order to steady up?"

"Sir, I thought—"

"You thought! You thought! You're not being paid to think!" the captain screeched. "You just do as you're goddam told and don't go thinking—please!"

The helmsman's legs were trembling. His face was white and his eyes seemed to be popping from his head. "Aye aye, sir," he gasped. "Shall I come left again—"

"Don't do ANYTHING!" Queeg screamed. "What course are you on?"

"Tu—tu—two-two-five, sir, coming right—"

"I thought you steadied on 220—"

"I stopped steadying, sir, when you said—"

"For Christ's sake will you stop telling me what I said? Now, you come left and steady on 220!!"

"Aye aye, sir, l-left and steady on 220."

"Mr. Maryk!" shouted the captain. The first lieutenant came running into the wheelhouse. "What's this man's name and rating?" . . .

"I want him relieved and I want an experienced man at this wheel hereafter when we're in the channel, not a green, stupid idiot—". . .

Willie Keith put his head in. "Something, looks like a battleship, dead ahead, Captain, three hundred yards!"

Queeg looked up in horror. A vast dark bulk was bearing down on the Caine. Queeg opened and closed his mouth three times without uttering a sound, then he choked out, "All engines back full—bah—bah—belay that—All stop."

The order had barely been countermanded when the battleship slipped down the starboard side of the Caine, hooting angrily with perhaps ten feet of open water between the hulls. It was like a steel cliff going by.

"Red channel buoy, one point port bow," called down a lookout from the flying bridge.

"No wonder," said Maryk to the captain. "We're on the wrong side of the channel, sir."

"We're not on the wrong side of anything," snapped the captain. "If you'll tend to your business and get another helmsman, I'll tend to my business and conn my ship, Mr. Maryk!"

I keep picturing all these little kids playing some game in this big field of rye and all. Thousands of little kids, and nobody's around —nobody big, I mean—except me. And I'm standing on the edge of some crazy cliff. What I have to do, I have to catch everybody if they start to go over the cliff —I mean if they're running *and they don't look where they're going I have to come out from somewhere and CATCH them. That's all I do all day. I'd just be the catcher in the rye and all. I know it's crazy but that's the only thing I'd really like to be. I know it's crazy."*

Old Phoebe didn't say anything for a long time. Then, when she said something, all she said was, "Daddy's going to kill you."

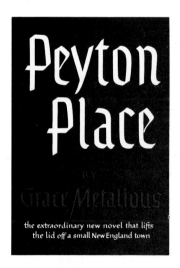

"Please," she whispered, and before he could move toward her she ran to him. "Please," she cried. "Please. Please."

And then he was holding her and his lips were against her cheek, at the corners of her eyes, soft against her ear as he murmured, "Darling, darling," while Constance wept.

Her finger tips traced a pattern down the side of his face, and with her mouth almost against his she whispered, "I didn't know it could be like this . . ."

She could not lie still under his hands.

"Anything," she said. "Anything. Anything."

"I love this fire in you. I love it when you have to move."

"Don't stop."

"Here? And here? And here?

"Yes. Oh, yes. Yes."

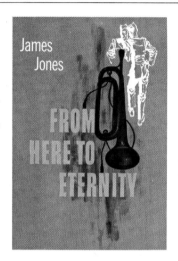

This is the song of the men who have no place, played by a man who has never had a place, and can therefore play it. Listen to it. You know this song, remember? This is the song you close your ears to every night, so you can sleep. This is the song you drink five martinis every evening not to hear. This is the song of the Great Loneliness, that creeps in like the desert wind and dehydrates the soul. This is the song you'll listen to on the day you die. When you lay there in the bed and sweat it out, and know that all the doctors and nurses and weeping friends dont mean a thing and cant help you any, cant save you one small bitter taste of it, because you are the one thats dying and not them; when you wait for it to come and know that sleep will not evade it and martinis will not put it off . . . then you will hear this song and, remembering, recognize it. This song is Reality. Remember? Surely you Remember?

> *"Day   is done . . .*
> *Gone   the sun . . .*
> *From-the-lake*
> *From-the-hill*
> *From-the-sky*
> *Rest in peace*
> *Sol jer brave*
> *God   is   nigh . . ."*

THE GREAT INSPIRATIONAL
BEST-SELLER OF OUR TIME

THE Power of Positive Thinking

NORMAN VINCENT PEALE

A PRACTICAL GUIDE TO MASTERING
THE PROBLEMS OF EVERYDAY LIVING

The EXURBANITES

BY A. C. SPECTORSKY

WITH DRAWINGS BY ROBERT OSBORN

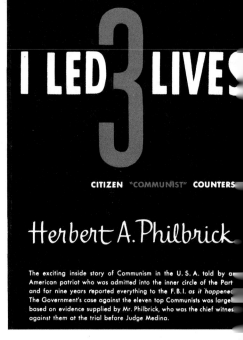

I LED 3 LIVES

CITIZEN "COMMUNIST" COUNTERS

Herbert A. Philbrick

The exciting inside story of Communism in the U.S.A. told by an American patriot who was admitted into the inner circle of the Party and for nine years reported everything to the F.B.I. *as it happened.* The Government's case against the eleven top Communists was largely based on evidence supplied by Mr. Philbrick, who was the chief witness against them at the trial before Judge Medina.

THE STATUS SEEKERS

AN EXPLORATION OF CLASS BEHAVIOR IN AMERICA AND THE HIDDEN BARRIERS THAT AFFECT YOU, YOUR COMMUNITY, YOUR FUTURE

VANCE PACKARD

AUTHOR OF "THE HIDDEN PERSUADERS"

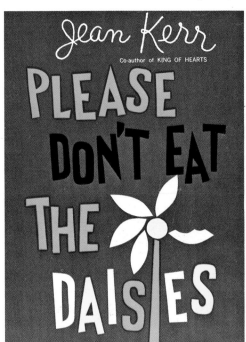

Jean Kerr
Co-author of KING OF HEARTS

PLEASE DON'T EAT THE DAISIES

SIX MEN CROSS THE PACIFIC ON A RAFT

KON-TIKI

BY THOR HEYERDAHL

A sampling of popular nonfiction reflects readers' taste for books that explore their own world. The subjects ranged from Thor Heyerd

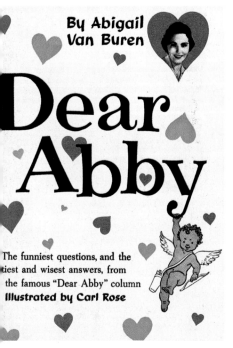

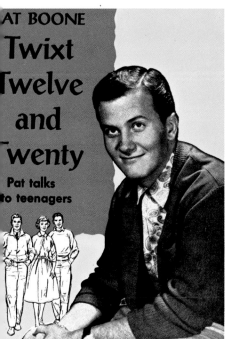

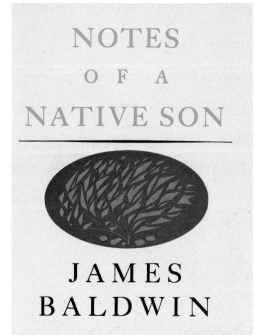

enturesome "Kon-Tiki" to James Baldwin's bitter look at the reality of being black.

The Bestsellers

Below are the top-selling books of the '50s with the number of copies each book sold in the year it led.

Fiction

1950 THE CARDINAL
Henry Morton Robinson—588,000

1951 FROM HERE TO ETERNITY
James Jones—240,000

1952 THE SILVER CHALICE
Thomas B. Costain—221,000

1953 THE ROBE
Lloyd C. Douglas—188,000

1954 NOT AS A STRANGER
Morton Thompson—178,000

1955 MARJORIE MORNINGSTAR
Herman Wouk—191,000

1956 DON'T GO NEAR THE WATER
William Brinkley—165,000

1957 BY LOVE POSSESSED
James Gould Cozzens—217,000

1958 DOCTOR ZHIVAGO
Boris Pasternak—500,000

1959 EXODUS
Leon Uris—400,000

Nonfiction

1950 BETTY CROCKER'S PICTURE
COOK BOOK
300,000

1951 LOOK YOUNGER, LIVE LONGER
Gaylord Hauser—287,000

1952 THE HOLY BIBLE:
Revised Standard Version
2,000,000

1953 THE HOLY BIBLE:
Revised Standard Version
1,100,000

1954 THE HOLY BIBLE:
Revised Standard Version
710,000

1955 GIFT FROM THE SEA
Anne Morrow Lindbergh—430,000

1956 ARTHRITIS AND COMMON SENSE,
Revised Edition
Dan Dale Alexander—255,000

1957 KIDS SAY THE DARNDEST THINGS!
Art Linkletter—175,000

1958 KIDS SAY THE DARNDEST THINGS!
Art Linkletter—225,000

1959 'TWIXT TWELVE AND TWENTY
Pat Boone—260,000

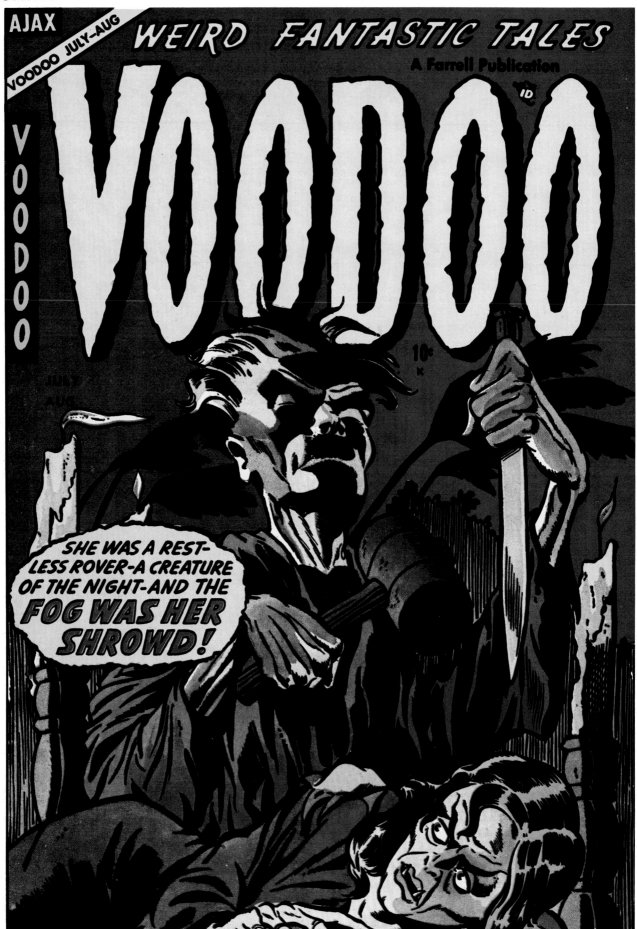

Besides serving up a brew of violence, horror books committed grisly spelling sins like putting a "w" in shroud.

Movie magazines paid respectful attention to the hundreds of letters that poured in monthly from their readers. In fact the letters went a long way toward determining the contents of the magazines. No matter how fatuous they sounded, 50 letters in one month mentioning Tab Hunter were reason enough to send editors scurrying to tell about Tab in print.

To make sure the letters kept coming, the magazines encouraged mail by every device short of paying out hard cash. *Modern Screen* invited queries for an intimate question-and-answer column at the level of "How old is Natalie Wood—really?" *Photoplay* ran a "Readers Inc." department; then, as an extra come-on, published a section in which Claudette Colbert *personally* solved the social problems of readers. As the letters below reveal, readers took their Hollywood seriously, commenting earnestly on its personalities and following the stars' fortunes with unflagging interest.

MODERN SCREEN, AUGUST 1956 *I think you had a hand in the reconciliation of the Dean Martins. You wrote an open letter in "Modern Screen" telling Dean and Jeanne how silly they were to stay apart when they really love one another. I read your words, and I bet they did, too.*

Maria, New York

SCREEN MAGAZINE, OCTOBER 1954 *Getting to my reason and favorite subject for this letter is Don O'Connor. The happy thought of seeing wonderful Don dance and sing, joke and woo lucky Janet Leigh makes my sad heart a little lighter. Don has always had the secret power to make me forget everything and just relax.*

B. W., Winchester, Illinois

PHOTOPLAY, MARCH 1958 *I enjoy "Photoplay" because of the pictures and articles about certain people. Before I read the article about Jayne Mansfield, I thought she was the sexiest actress in Hollywood, but now I realize differently. After I read the article told by her mother in the December issue of "Photoplay," I realized that she's just like any other girl off the screen. I was ashamed of what I thought of her and I only wish that more teenagers and adults would read the articles in "Photoplay" about certain stars they have the wrong impression about.*

L. A., Superior, Wis.

PHOTOPLAY, AUGUST 1955
There may be many imitators
But really no originators.
Six feet tall, minus two
Eyes are gray with specks of blue.
He laughs, he cries, smiles and screams
But whatever he does his public beams.
As Napoleon, Zapata, or even a bum
He's terrific, colossal, as great as they come.
For we, the fans, think he's just grand.
From the pick of the tops, Marlon's our brand
(Brando!)

C. B. and S. C., Toronto, Canada

PHOTOPLAY, JULY 1950 *Why doesn't Farley Granger get wise to himself and lay off that Shelley Winters and pay more attention to pretty Joan Evans?*

Y. Q., Detroit, Mich.

Intriguing Foreigners

As more and more Americans stayed home in the '50s to watch TV, Hollywood slackened its bustling pace and thousands of neighborhood movie palaces turned into supermarkets. The theaters that remained faced a dearth of films, forcing exhibitors to turn overseas for what Hollywood had customarily supplied. With subtitles added (often in fractured or dreadfully flat English), the foreign film invaded the American market in such numbers that U.S. earnings for imports rose approximately 500 per cent between 1956 and 1960.

The audience for these movies knew exactly what it wanted, and at decade's end the nation's favorite foreign actress was French "sex kitten" Brigitte Bardot. In a series of wide-screen full-color, lightweight movies, "B.B." wriggled and pouted and doffed her clothes for the casually wrapped sheet or towel that one critic called her badge. Of all the Bardot movies released in the U.S., *And God Created Woman*

made the most money (four million dollars' gross on an investment of $400,000) and aroused the most controversy *(below)*. In some cities it ran for months at art theaters that normally showed films for only a few weeks at a time, while in other cities (Philadelphia, Fort Worth, Abilene, Memphis, Providence) it was banned.

But there was more to foreign films *(following pages)* than the attraction of Bardot, and slowly these other qualities created an enthusiastic following—mostly on college campuses and in big cities. Devotees of these attractions rarely went to the "movies" but often attended "films" or "the cinema," and the names that mattered on the marquee were those of film directors. Reviewing *Hiroshima, Mon Amour* when it opened in New York, *Esquire* movie critic Dwight Macdonald observed that the audience was "extraordinarily quiet—no coughing, whispering. . . . It was oddly like a religious service." The movies as an art had arrived.

A nd God Created Woman" is an assault on each and every woman of our community and nation, living or dead—our mothers, sisters, wives and daughters.

THE REVEREND JAMES T. LYNG, LAKE PLACID, NEW YORK

The people of Philadelphia don't want this type of film. In my opinion, it's dirt for dirt's sake.

ASSISTANT DISTRICT ATTORNEY M. R. HALBERT

"And God Created Woman" opens with a shot that promises a good deal more than the picture delivers. There lies Brigitte, stretched from end to end of the CinemaScope screen, bottoms up and bare as a censor's

eyeball. In the hard sun of the Riviera her little round rear glows like a peach, and the camera lingers on the subject as if waiting for it to ripen. If sex is the object, there is just about as much to be seen in almost any Hollywood film, and in promulgating Brigitte as a full-blown enchantress, the French have clearly sent a girl to do a woman's job.

TIME, NOVEMBER 11, 1957

We asked them not to show it here.

MRS. RODERIC B. THOMAS, DALLAS, TEXAS

Lewd, obscene and lascivious.

WILLIAM J. GILLESPIE, LUBBOCK, TEXAS

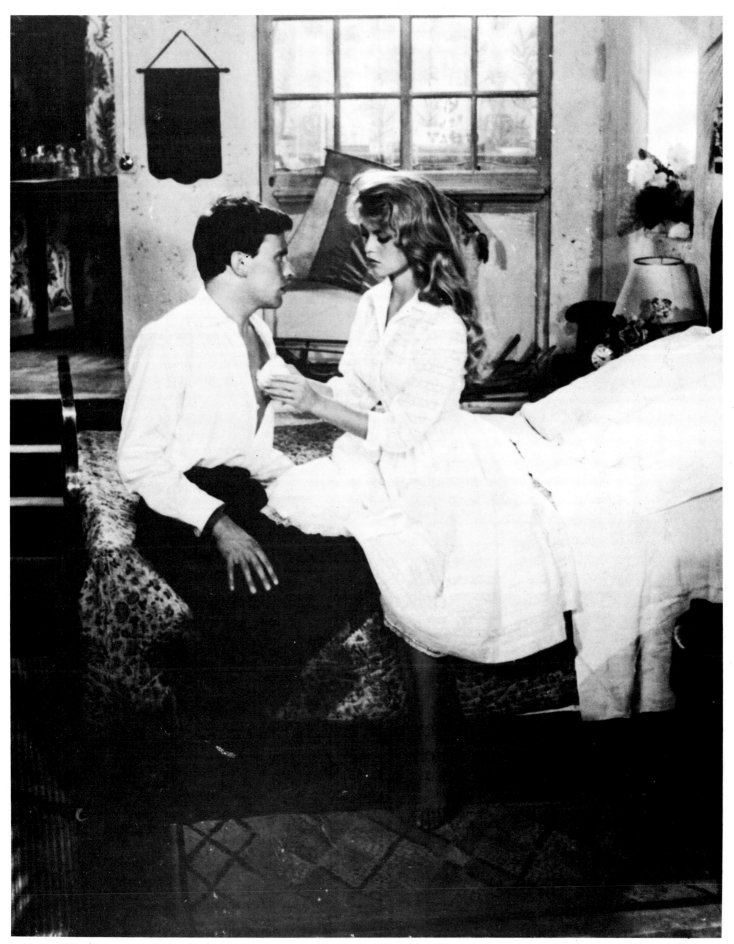

La Bardot coos to her wounded mate (played by Jean-Louis Trintignant) in a scene from the 1957 hit "And God Created Woman."

Culture

1958   BLACK ORPHEUS   France

1952   MR. HULOT'S HOLIDAY   Fran

1956   THE SEVENTH SEAL   Sweden

1959   HIROSHIMA, MON AMOUR   Fran

1954   LA STRADA   Italy

1957   THE CRANES ARE FLYING   Soviet Un

THE LAVENDER HILL MOB England

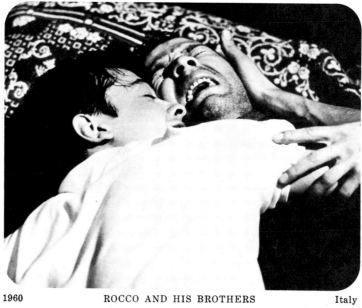

1960 ROCCO AND HIS BROTHERS Italy

THE WORLD OF APU India

1958 THE 400 BLOWS France

RASHOMON Japan

1959 ROOM AT THE TOP England

Fierce Fun with Human Foibles

A new brand of comedy emerged in the mid-'50s. It was sharp, satirical *(following pages)* and several light-years removed from the set-piece gags of Jack Benny and Fibber McGee.

At first, a nation reared on mother-in-law jokes was baffled and upset by the grim subject matter of the new humor and defensively labeled it "sick." The word was picked up with instant delight and used for a book title by Jules Feiffer, the leading cartoonist among the new comedians *(right)*.

But basically the '50s humor contained the very essence of health, for it probed and exposed some of the annoying viruses in modern life: pompous and prejudiced politicians, pretentious movies and books, nauseating television commercials and a host of other absurdities and confusions.

Most important of all, the new humor was often hilariously funny. Mike Nichols, who with his equally gifted partner Elaine May contrived some of the most convulsing spoofs of all, could undo with a single line the clichéd pretensions of bad Southern writing. Posing as a Deep-South playwright named Alabama Gross, Nichols described the fate of the heroine in his hypo-

thetical new drama: She has "taken to drink, dope, prostitution—and puttin' on airs." The last phrase was delivered in a rising, quizzical tenor, devastatingly similar to the lecture-hall style of Tennessee Williams.

With a similar, acid-tipped dart, Mort Sahl commented on Eisenhower's frequent golfing trips: "I wondered if it was legally possible to get a Taft-Hartley injunction which would force the President to stay in the White House for 80 consecutive days."

Shelley Berman, a gentler comedian, could still raise welts on his listeners' psyches, as when he wondered why, if dental X-rays were so safe, the dentist, having aimed the buzzing machine at your jaw, retreated into the next room.

As for Feiffer, he probed gently but inexorably in his cartoon panels at the moral, psychological and sexual confusions of a generation that was under the influence of a brew of ill-understood Freud, decayed religion and cast-iron platitudes. As the cartoons *(right)* from his book *Sick, Sick, Sick* demonstrate, Feiffer was a worthy successor to James Thurber in anatomizing what the older humorist called "the war between the sexes."

The case of Mort Sahl shows that one of the heaviest influences on American humor is the changing political climate. He rose because of Eisenhower. How desperately we needed Sahl's voice during those bland years. Looking back now on the Eisenhower era, it seems painfully clear that the nation fell into an eight-year sleep. McCarthyism and fear were allowed to flourish; civil rights decisions were passed and then conspicuously not enforced; culture and the arts were starved. But we were not told much about any of this, and we didn't want to be told. We just wanted Ike to assure us that everything was O.K., which he did, and we rolled over and went back to sleep.

Mort Sahl, however, stayed awake, and his response when he found that the whole country was under sedation—which he correctly felt was dangerous—was angry and bitter. As if by some natural law, the most insipid administration provoked the most acid reaction.

CRITIC WILLIAM K. ZINSSER

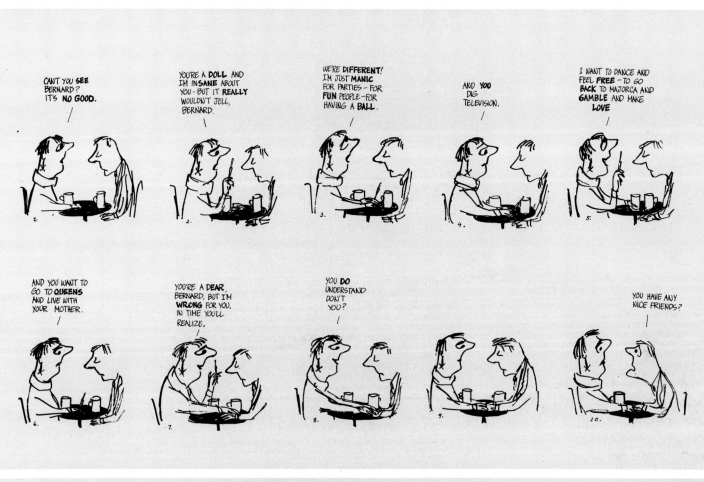

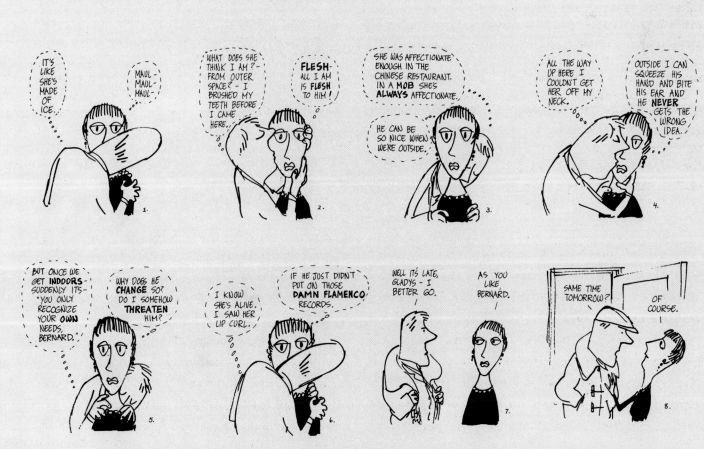

Two Feiffer anti-heroes seek their fates from a pair of nonaffectionate women in these chillingly funny Feiffer versions of modern love.

Berman speaks into his favorite prop, an imaginary telephone.

Shelley Berman

The comic forte of Shelley Berman was making comedy out of "the very small type of embarrassing moment" —as when a goodnight kiss lands off center and "you wind up with the tip of her nose in the corner of your mouth." A trained actor, he did lengthy routines that were almost playlets, moving from the plausible to the ridiculous. Below is an abridged version of Berman's skit about life in a modern, claustrophobic hotel room.

Hello, desk clerk? Berman—Room 702. I just checked in. No, everything is all right. I just—I want to ask about one thing. I don't seem to have a window. No, I looked. No, I looked over there, too. No, there's nothing specific I want to see; it's just I'd like a window if I could get a hold of one. Well, I didn't think to request a window when I booked the room. I thought for sure I'd have one. I just feel a man should have a window.

No, there's plenty of hot water—loads of hot water. As a matter of fact, from both taps. One sort of curious thing, sir. You know the dresser—four drawers? Three are painted on. Now why is that?

Well, now that's the other thing I want to ask you about, sir. I—I can't find my door, sir. I'm not denying I have a door. I'm in the room. There must be a door. I didn't materialize in here, but I cannot find the damn door! Now where do you think I'd find it? Near which window? I don't have a window. Wouldn't that be an odd place to put a door—next to a window? I mean, if you walked through you'd fall out of the building. I have one door over here, but that's the door to my closet. Oh, I thought I had one. Well maybe that's the door to my bathroom. You're kidding! Well, where is it? I don't need a pencil, just tell me how to find it!

Mort Sahl

Among the young critic-comedians, Morton Lyon Sahl was the most relentless harrier of the nation's political follies. He spattered his largely ad-lib monologues with irreverent attacks on half of Washington. He never did a set "routine"; instead he built seemingly haphazard structures of mordant musings and swift barbs. Below is a sampling of the often weirdly angled shafts he let fly during his nightclub appearances in the 1950s.

ON PRESIDENT EISENHOWER'S FONDNESS FOR GOLF: *If you are in the Administration, you have a lot of problems of policy, like whether or not to use an overlapping grip.*

ON THE UN-AMERICAN ACTIVITIES COMMITTEE: *Every time the Russians throw an American in jail, the committee throws an American in jail to get even.*

ON ESPIONAGE AND THE SO-CALLED MISSILE GAP: *Maybe the Russians will steal all our secrets. Then they'll be two years behind.*

ON THE VAST POWER OF U.S. BIG BUSINESS: *One of these days General Motors is going to get sore and cut the Government off without a penny. . . . The Chase Manhattan Bank has several subsidiaries, you know—Western Germany, for one.*

ON PRESIDENT-ELECT JOHN F. KENNEDY'S AGE: *You know, Kennedy had to have Lyndon Johnson on the ticket with him because he can't get into Washington without an adult.*

ON HIMSELF: *I'm the intellectual voice of the era—which is a good measure of the era.*

Nervous hands fluttering, Sahl fires away in his staccato style.

Nichols and May

The poet laureates of the fatuous were Nichols and May, whose wide-eyed good looks camouflaged a buzz-saw sense of satire. Their superbly timed ad-lib duets held up the human race on a pin and made it laugh while it squirmed. Their targets included addled P.T.A. committeewomen, classical music snobs, American sexual guilt. The excerpt below is from their skit on a British dentist who falls in love with his patient.

MAY: *When I first came into your office, when I saw you standing there so stern in your white smock, I thought, he loathes me for having a cavity.*

NICHOLS: *Oh no I didn't, because it was YOUR cavity and I think even then I loved it. There, I've said it. Let's not talk about it for just a minute. (Pause)*

MAY: *When you looked into my mouth and said, "It's rotten," I thought nothing can happen to me now. But when you looked at me, you didn't look at me as though I were a woman with a rotten tooth. You looked at me as though I were Me!*

NICHOLS: *Oh, Reba, Reba—When I first looked into that mouth and saw that you were English clear through, I think I knew then that something I didn't mean to happen was going to happen. I have something I have to tell you, Reba. I'm going away. I've taken a job as a dentist in a leper colony. I think it's best.*

MAY: *I think that it's the right choice. I think there are good lepers and bad lepers—you can't lump them together. . . . I'm going away, too. I'm going to Saudi Arabia to become a dental assistant.*

NICHOLS: *Reba, you know nothing about teeth!*

MAY: *I know, but I can learn. If I could teach just one Saudi Arabian the rules of dental hygiene. . . .*

Nichols as a pompous, name-dropping disk jockey ("My old friend Albert Schweitzer") interviews May as a vacuous sex-bomb.

Rebels

A motorcyclist in the standard garb of his club munches an ear of corn.

The Wild Ones

There was no wilder, gayer girl in the crowd that tagged after the Cobras than Lucille.

Bebop was her boy friend and she kept his piece, a nickle-plated revolver, hidden in a box

under her bed. Lucille was fifteen last summer and it was the best summer of her life.

HARRISON SALISBURY IN *THE SHOOK-UP GENERATION*

During the first half of the '50s, teenagers showed the same low, unalarming profile they had presented in the '40s, but by mid-decade the first dark shoots of rebellion began to sprout in big-city slums. In New York during 1956, the number of teen-age murderers was up 26 per cent over the previous year. Teenagers were largely responsible for the 36 per cent increase in auto thefts and the 92 per cent jump in possession of dangerous weapons. The challenge to adult authority spread to rural areas and suburban neighborhoods. But the majority of teen rebels, including those shown on these pages, looked more dangerous than they were. Police estimated that only one in every 10 gangs in New York, Chicago or Los Angeles was actively violent; and across the country less than 1 per cent of the adolescent population had ever been hauled in on criminal charges.

Yet the outer trappings of the delinquent gang became symbols of revolt for kids on all economic levels. They adopted the black-leather jackets *(right)* and tight jeans of real hoods, talked a lingo derived from bebop, decorated themselves with tattoos (some painted on rather than needle-set, the easier to remove) and ran with tousle-haired girls whose clothing was identical to the boys'. They flocked to movies like *The Wild One,* in which Marlon Brando played the "president" of a satanic troop of cycle riders; *High School Confidential,* in which a young hood asks an enemy, "You got 32 teeth, wanna try for none?"; and *Teenage Doll,* a grisly drama about gang warfare that bore the opening warning, "This is not a pretty story, but it is true."

No one knows how or why the rebellion started, but everyone had his own pet theory. Pennsylvania policemen said it was all due to rock and roll tunes, terming them "more suggestive than those sung in burlesque houses." The venerable cartoon *Little Orphan Annie* devoted itself to a "penetrating analysis of teen-age violence" in 1956, whereupon the *St. Louis Globe Democrat* dropped the strip for showing too many "muggings, switchblade knives and language that we think does not fit into this type of newspaper." A more valuable contribution toward understanding of the teen-age rebel was made by *New York Times* reporter Harrison Salisbury in his book, *The Shook-Up Generation (pages 246-247).* The slang and quotations on the following pages are from conversations that Salisbury had with kids he interviewed in the course of writing that book.

Two youths mind their turf: "What do I want to do in life? Stay alive. Some people say I won't live so long."

Rolling his shirt sleeves to the prescribed height, a "big

rson" waits to get moving while his chick fixes her hair: "One thing I'll tell you, I'm going to get out of this dump. And never come back."

*A crouching bopper taunts a rival (above), while a
window-shopper (right) looks over a selection of
switchblades: "You take Chico. He has more heart
than anyone I ever saw. He's crazy, that boy. . . . Once we
had a rumble with the Chaplains. You know what
he did? He went out alone right into Chaplains' turf. In
daylight. Just walked in, inviting them to jap him
. . . He'll fight anybody. . . . Man, he sure have heart."*

Leaning on a roadhouse jukebox, a g

lks with her boyfriend, "What do you like to read?" "Nothin'. I don't like to read." "What do you like to do?" "Sit." "Just sit?" "Just sit."

Four studs scan the scene looking for date material,
while a luckier brother (right) starts to make it with his chick:
"Nothing was going on that night and that's a fact.
It was too hot to do anything. We didn't have any plans."

"You go steady and first thing she wants you
to spend all your time with her . . . to stop fighting.
She's afraid you get hurt. She starts talking that marriage stuff.
None of that going steady for me."

The president revs his cycle as the gang falls in behind: "A lea

s to have a sense of responsibility for his men. . . . I give my men orders. . . . Don't start anything. The cops are just waiting to pick you up.''

In his study of adolescent gangs, *The Shook-Up Generation,* Harrison Salisbury drew a sympathetic picture of a New York slum society that strangely resembled the world of medieval knights. Like knights, hoods donned ritual armor (leather jackets that helped deflect enemy knife thrusts) before jousting with one another, or "bopping." The boys assumed heraldic nicknames that contained a great deal of unconscious poetry: Geronimo, Snake, Diablo, Hatchet, Saint. The names of the gangs themselves also summoned up images worthy of the old sagas: Vikings, Centurions, Crusaders, Viceroys. One club member explained the motto of his organization was "All for one, and one for all," a slogan borrowed directly from the 17th Century Musketeers.

In the violent world of gang life, as in the ancient world of chivalry, the most prized quality was reckless, even suicidal, courage, which the kids called "heart." If a gang member was killed in action, the survivors shrugged it off with a stoic cliché: "That's the way the little ball bounces." But when gang members passed the dead boy's house, they put their hats over their hearts in silent tribute. These and other aspects of street-gang life—its private language and peculiar rituals—are described by Salisbury in the excerpts below.

As far as the Cobras know . . . the gang has always been there. No Cobra can imagine his world, or any world, without a street gang.

You can meet the Cobras any day of the week from four o'clock on in the afternoon. That is the hour when they begin to collect outside Schroeder's candy store. . . . Winter, spring or summer you will see them in this same spot—teetering back and forth, heel-to-toe, loose-jointed, shoulders hunched a little, hands deep thrust in trousers' pockets, heads and chins bobbing and darting, duckfashion, eyes quick to detect any stranger. . . .

The Cobras are protecting their demesne—"minding our turf," in the argot of the streets. With a little time out for dinner some of them will stand on that corner until 11 P.M. of a winter's night, regardless of cold, and until 1 or 2 A.M. (unless chased away by the police) on sultry summer evenings. . . .

Most of the Cobras happen to be Negro. They live, play, work and fight beside and in close relation with a "brother club," the Silver Arrows, whose membership is largely Puerto Rican. The racial divisions closely follow those of the population of the Whitman Housing Project. . . . The Cobras and Arrows are "tight" in the language of the streets. This means they are close allies in the treacherous, shifting sphere of the bop. . . . When they look beyond the boundaries of the Whitman project they see a dark and dangerous jungle.

Within this sea of danger exist two well-known, well-identified enemies—the Rovers (Irish-Italian) and the Apaches (largely Irish). . . . The conflict between the Cobras and the Arrows, on the one hand, and the Rovers and the Apaches on the other has roots so twisted that none of the teenagers can tell the story straight. The enmity is as deep, bitter and tortuous as any feud in Montenegro. . . .

The Cobras divide themselves into two categories —Big People and Little People. . . . Big People are sixteen to nineteen, for the most part. They are the core of the fighting gang. Little People are younger, ranging from nine or ten to about fifteen. . . .

The Cobras are what social workers call a "struc- tured" gang. That is, they have a leadership clique with titles, offices and responsibilities—a President (public policy, domestic and foreign relations, strategy), a Vice-President (Chief of Staff and Second in Com- mand), a War Counselor (war plans, intelligence, tactics); and a Gunsmith or Armorer (weapons and lo- gistics). The Little People have a similar top echelon but are subordinate to overall control by the Big People.

When a strange boy walks past the Cobra candy store the following conversation may ensue:

"Who you swinging with, man?"

"Why, I'm swinging with the Bishops, man."

"Good, man. We're tight with the Bishops. We're a brother club. How about dropping a dime, man, and we'll get a bottle of sneaky pete."

"Okay, man. I thought you might be shaking me down."

"Oh, you figured you might have to shuffle, eh?"

"That's what I thought, man. But I'm telling you I got a piece on me. Nobody going to jap me, man."

"I thought you might be a coolie, man."

"You trying to sound me? Let's get that sneaky pete and have us a gig."

Or, in English:

"What street club do you belong to?"

"I belong to the Bishops."

"Good, we're friendly with the Bishops. They are af- filiated with our club. How about contributing a dime toward a bottle of wine?"

"Okay, I was afraid you would try to hold me up."

"You thought you might have to fight?"

"Yes, that's why I'm carrying a gun. I'm not letting anyone take me by surprise."

"I thought you might not belong to a gang."

"Don't kid me. Let's get that wine and have a party."

At a little after nine the gangs were ready. The Cobras and Arrows had their weapons . . . and the Bishops and Stompers were arriving in twos or threes. . . . They did not congregate on the street corner but dispersed in small knots and moved toward the Rovers' turf. As they slipped through the drowsy streets some boys snapped radio aerials off parked cars. The aerials are a deadly weapon. Wielded as a steel whip they can lay a face open to the bone. Used as a spear they will penetrate the lungs or stomach.

As the Cobras neared Beaver Street they could hear the wail of the jukeboxes. In the distance thunder re- verberated. Suddenly came a ragged fusillade of shots and the roar of motors. The rumble was on. The cars raced to the end of Beaver Street, spun on whining tires and whirled back for a second pass at the stunned Rov- ers. Glass shattered as shots broke store-front windows. . . . Four and five youngsters jumped on each of the Rovers, beating the boys to the ground, stabbing with knives, flailing with steel rods, stomping with their boots. Beaver Street was a turmoil of shouts, cries for help, screams of pain. . . . Then, in the distance, came the moan of a police siren. As suddenly as they had de- scended the Cobras and their allies fled.

Television

TV's top guns open fire: (from left) Cheyenne, of "Cheyenne"; Matt Dillon, "Gunsmoke"; Paladin, "Have Gun, Will Travel"; Flint McCullough, "Wagon Train"; Bret Maverick, "Maverick"; Vint Bonner, "Restless Gun."

The Electronic Opiate

Television is a triumph of equipment over people, and the minds that control it are so small that you could put them in the navel of a flea and still have enough room beside them for a network vice-president's heart.

FRED ALLEN

When General of the Army Dwight D. Eisenhower called a press conference in Abilene, Kansas, in June 1952 to announce his candidacy for President of the United States, a regiment of radio and newspapermen crushed around him to hear his words, while a small band of television cameras stood outside in the rain. To film the event for the home screen, cameraman Jesse Zousmer of CBS had to ram himself and his gear through the door. The rest of the newsmen howled that TV was usurping their special function and labeled the incident the Battle of Abilene.

When that battle was waged in 1952, the faces that generally dominated the nation's TV screens were vaudeville and radio comedians like Milton Berle *(opposite)*, who brought the guffaws of vaudeville into the living room. Many Americans believed that such fare was all the tube was good for. Intellectuals made a fetish of not owning an "idiot box"; preachers thundered that TV would corrupt the morals of the young. One movie tycoon, alarmed that theater attendance was dropping by the millions, said with more hope than foresight: "Video isn't able to hold onto the market it captures after the first six months. People soon get tired of staring at a plywood box every night."

But the fact was that television was in the process of dominating the communications industry. In 1950 there were TV sets in only 3.1 million U.S. homes. Halfway through the decade, the figure had jumped to 32 million. By the end of another year, Americans had spent $15.6 billion to buy sets and keep them repaired.

For all its eager acceptance by the people, TV continued to evoke much condemnation. It was called "the boob tube" and "the light that failed." Some of the down-talking came from veteran performers who never managed to make the switch from radio to the new medium. One such was Fred Allen, who uttered the rueful words inscribed above. Other criticism came from newsman Edward R. Murrow *(pages 268-269)*, himself the decade's top TV commentator. "If television and radio are to be used for the entertainment of all of the people all of the time," he said, "we have come perilously close to discovering the real opiate of the people." Opiate it very nearly was. By 1959 the average U.S. family was sitting before the box some six hours a day, seven days a week. Some samples of what they watched with such fascination appear on the following pages.

Funnyman Milton Berle, known as "Mr. Television," kept millions glued to their TV sets on Tuesday nights for more than six years.

The indefatigable Lucy takes up ballet dancing—only to get herself trapped on the bar while her teacher looks on in helpless dismay.

Everybody Loved Lucy

*Perhaps the zaniest and most
popular show of the decade was "I Love Lucy," a
spoof of married life starring
movie actress Lucille Ball and her Cuban-born
bandleader husband, Desi Arnaz. At
the end of its first six months of life, in 1952,
"Lucy" displaced Milton
Berle and Arthur Godfrey from top rating; less than
a year later its stars signed a contract for
eight million dollars, the biggest ever written in
TV. More people watched Lucy
mugging on Monday nights in January 1953 than
saw President Eisenhower's
inauguration in the same month, and the show
went on to lure an audience of 50 million viewers.*

Lucy's husband throws a fit.

Lucy makes ready to throw a pie.

She dances with neighbor Ethel.

Situation Comedies

THE HONEYMOONERS

DOBIE GILLIS

OZZIE AND HARRIET

THE PHIL SILVERS SHOW

FATHER KNOWS BEST

LEAVE IT TO BEAVER

DECEMBER BRIDE

BURNS AND ALLEN SHOW

MR. PEEPERS

OUR MISS BROOKS

MAKE ROOM FOR DADDY

MAMA

Mugging furiously, Sid Caesar and Imogene Coca do a spoof on Rudolf Valentino's famous love movie of the '20s, "The Sheik."

Satirizing the British stiff upper lip, Caesar, Coca and friends sit oblivious to the torrents of rain from a leaky castle roof.

The Perils of Saturday Night

In 1954, after 160 performances, Sid Caesar's
superb revue "Your Show of Shows"—co-starring Imogene Coca, ably
abetted by Carl Reiner and Howard Morris (above)—died of
exposure and rising production costs. The wise money along Madison Avenue
nodded smugly at the demise and dredged up the old
vaudeville slogan, "Satire is what closes on Saturday night." For "Show" had
not only focused on satire but had run as a Saturday night feature.
One of the best remembered skits was "From Here to Obscurity" (excerpted overleaf), a
burlesque of the film version of "From Here to Eternity."

Carl Reiner smashes Sid Caesar's bugle in their satire of "From Here to Eternity." At right is Howard Morris.

FROM HERE TO OBSCURITY

SCENE: *An orderly room on an Army base in Hawaii. Cast: Sid Caesar as Private Montgomery Bugle; Carl Reiner as top sergeant; Howard Morris as a private; Imogene Coca as a dancehall girl.*
REINER: *(On phone)* Yes, Captain Wilson. No, Captain Wilson. But I promise we won't lose the next matches. Yes, sir. *(Hangs up)* *(To Morris)* Boy, is the Captain mad. This is the first year Company E has lost the boxing matches. Some company I got this year. A bunch of creampuffs. Well, don't worry. I'm having a guy transferred here—the best boxer in the U.S. Army. *(Indicating papers)* He's due in today.
MORRIS: That guy. I know him. He's an old buddy of mine. He won't fight.

He refuses to get into the boxing ring.
REINER: Why?
MORRIS: Cuz he's a bugler. That's his whole life. He's never without a bugle.
REINER: In this outfit he's gonna be a boxer—or else.
MORRIS: Not him. All he wants to do is bugle. *(Sound offstage of bugle music. Enter Caesar, playing bugle)*
CAESAR: *(Seeing Morris)* Buddy boy—
MORRIS: Buddy boy. How are you?
CAESAR: Hi there, buddy boy, pal.
REINER: Attention! What's your name?
CAESAR: My name happens to be Montgomery Bugle.
REINER: Rank?
CAESAR: Nothing.
REINER: Okay, Private Bugle. Put that

bugle away. You won't need it in this outfit. You'll be a boxer now.
CAESAR: Excuse me, Sergeant. I didn't join the Army to fight. I joined up to blow the bugle. I'm the best bugler in the whole Army. *(Picks up bugle. Plays "You Made Me Love You")*
REINER: Gimme that. *(Tears bugle from Caesar and mangles it)* You're gonna be a boxer or you'll be sorry. *(Exits)*
CAESAR: *(Quietly picks up broken bugle, looks at it sadly, and plays it as beautifully as ever)* It's okay.
MORRIS: Monty, don't be stubborn, cuz if the Sarge wants you to be a boxer, he can make you be a boxer. Ever heard of The Treatment? *(Music)* They make it so tough for you, they'll have you beg-

ging to be a boxer.

CAESAR: I can't.

MORRIS: Why not?

CAESAR: Cuz a man is a person and a person has dignity and a man's got to have dignity in his heart. Then he'll have dignity, confidence and respect and dignity in my bugle. I ain't fighting.

MORRIS: But why, why?

CAESAR: Promise not to tell anyone?

MORRIS: Sure.

CAESAR: Well, a long time ago I was matched with my best buddy. He was my best pal. And on top of that he was my brother. I get into the ring with him. I try not to hit him. But all of a sudden he gave me a shot. I lost my entire head. Hit him right in the eye. I broke my hand. What a hard eyeball he had. So I ain't fighting any more. I may break my hand and then I can't hold my bugle.

REINER: *(Enters)* Okay, Bugle. Are you gonna box or would you rather get—The Treatment? *(Ominous music)*

CAESAR: I ain't boxing.

REINER: Okay, you asked for it. Before I get through, you'll beg to be a boxer.

MORRIS: Boy, he's gonna get The Treatment. I can't watch. *(Exits)*

REINER: Fall in for inspection. All right. Just look at you. Your Good Conduct Medal is all crooked. I'll straighten it. *(Digs it into him)* Look at your shoes. *(Stamps on his foot. Grinds foot)* This is only a sample of what you'll get if you don't box. Think it over. *(Exits)*

MORRIS: *(Enters)* Hey buddy boy, are you all right? What did he do to you?

CAESAR: *(Small voice)* He ain't so tough. If that's The Treatment, I can take anything he can dish out.

MORRIS: Great, good for you, buddy boy. We got an overnight pass. Let's catch the bus into town.

CAESAR: Yeah, just a minute till I get this medal out of my chest.

SCENE: *Crowded dance hall. Couples dancing very close, among them Reiner.*

MORRIS: *(Enters)* Hi fellas. *(To girl)* Hey, baby, how about a dance?

GIRL: All right.

MORRIS: Here's my ticket. *(They dance)* I got my buddy boy coming soon. He's changing into civvies. I want you should introduce him to a nice girl.

GIRL: Okay.

(Sound of trumpet: "You Made Me Love You." Enter Caesar wearing loud shirt, playing hot bugle. When he quits, mouthpiece sticks to his lips)

CAESAR AND MORRIS: Hello, buddy boy. *(Music: chord. Enter Coca, a sexy dancing girl. All eyes on her)*

CROWD: That's the Duchess. That's her. Some dame. What a looker. How about a dance, Duchess? I saw her first.

REINER: She dances with me.

COCA: Take it easy, boys. There's enough for everybody. *(To Reiner)* All right, big boy. Where's your ticket?

REINER: Here. *(They dance)* Duchess, you're wonderful.

COCA: I know.

REINER: You're gorgeous.

COCA: You're telling me.

REINER: I love you.

COCA: Who doesn't.

REINER: You're mine. All mine.

COCA: I'm yours. All yours.

(They dance very close. Sweet trumpet music is heard, muted. Coca is drawn to the music, as if hypnotized.)

COCA: You're a funny one. *(With passion)* I love you. *(Pawing him)* Suddenly life is worth living. I love you.

CAESAR: Okay, Duchess. Let's dance.

COCA: Sorry, you gotta have a ticket. No ticket. No dancing.

CAESAR: I want to be near you.

COCA: You're a funny one. You're mine. I'm yours. When I love a man, I love. I'm a one-man woman.

ENTER STRANGER: Hiya, Duchess. *(Kisses her on lips. She responds)* Don't forget our four o'clock date tomorrow.

COCA: Right.

CAESAR: What's going on here? I thought you were a one-man woman.

COCA: You're a funny one. I show you that you're the only man I love. *(Embraces him. Cracking metal is heard. Caesar takes out flattened bugle from his shirt)*

CAESAR: My best bugle! Boy, that's love. Why don't we get out of here?

COCA: You're right. Let's go swimming.

CAESAR: Yeah. . . .

SCENE: *Beach. Enter Coca, then Caesar wearing an inner tube.*

CAESAR: Darling! *(Drops inner tube)*

COCA: You're a funny one. Let's sit out here. Isn't the ocean beautiful?

CAESAR: Sort of makes me feel as if we're very close to each other.

COCA: That's just the feeling I have. On this beach tonight I can forget the dance hall. *(Water splashes her)*

CAESAR: I can forget my troubles too.

COCA: Monty, I love you. *(Splash)*

CAESAR: I was waiting for an eternity to hear those words. You know, here tonight amongst the ocean I don't see the hard dancing girl anymore. I just see a wonderful girl who is lost, and I'm going to help you find yourself. *(Splash)*

COCA: *(Fighting splashes)* Monty, I used to dream of a knight in shining armor *(Splash)* who would sweep me off my feet *(Splash)* and take me to a romantic castle *(Splash)*, but I don't want to dream anymore. I've found you.

CAESAR: Duchess, we haven't known each other for any length of time but there's something I've got to ask you.

COCA: Yes, Monty?

CAESAR: Did you bring a towel? *(Splash)*

SCENE: *The dance hall. Everybody is drunk and noisy.*

REINER: The Duchess is my girl and nobody is making time with my girl.

MORRIS: My buddy boy is making time with her right now. You're a has-been!

REINER: *(Lunging at Morris)* Why, you little weasel! If I see that Bugle with my girl I'll kill him! I'll kill him!

(Enter Caesar and Coca. Everybody looks at them. They walk to Reiner)

CAESAR: Oh, yeah? Who you gonna kill?

REINER: *(Takes a bottle and breaks it)* You, wise guy!

CAESAR: *(Picks up bottle)* Okay, you asked for it. *(Tries to break bottle but it doesn't break. Coca takes bottle. She can't break it either)*

REINER: *(Throws bottle away, pulls gun)* Okay, Bugle. It's taps for you.

CAESAR: Now you show your true colors, Sarge. *(Caesar grabs gun and they tussle back and forth, each one doing a frightened take as gun barrel points at him)* You won't get away with that!

REINER: Is that so?

(In desperation Caesar bends barrel of gun back towards Reiner. Gun falls to floor. They both go for it. Caesar gets it)

CAESAR: Okay, Sarge, you asked for it. *(He laughs and fires, shooting himself. He pauses in amazement, looks down at himself)* Why should it hurt me more than it did him? *(He starts to figure it out)* The bullet went in here—went down and around—oh-ho-ho-ho and it came out here. *(He stares at it, disgusted)* What a blunder! *(He dies)* *(Coca sadly takes lei from Morris and drops it on Caesar)*

COCA: He was a funny one! *(She takes the bugle and blows it)*

THE END

Affable moderator John Daly grins at "What's My Line?" regulars and off-and-on guest panelist Steve Allen.

The Career of "What's My Line?"

It was a pretty silly formula. A man or woman, called a challenger, would enter the studio and "sign in" on a blackboard. Then words would flash on the screen telling the audience what the challenger did for a living. The job was always far out—one man put sticks in popsicles, another sold church steeples, still another polished jelly beans. Then four panelists, using the old 20-Questions technique, would try to guess the occupation.

Despite this simple-minded format—or because of it—*What's My Line?* outlasted all other quiz shows at a time when quizzes were one of TV's staples. The particular appeal of *What's My Line?* lay in the regular members of the panel, a carefully mixed bag that, during the show's 17½-year run, changed hardly at all. There was quince-faced Dorothy Kilgallen, who asked the sharpest questions; cheerful and feminine Arlene Francis, who often guessed on impulse; and owlish Bennett Cerf, whose penchant for overripe puns (a cow that swallowed ink "mood indigo") camouflaged the fact that he was the shrewd chief of one of the nation's top publishing houses. They were joined by a fourth panelist, usually a well-known comedian. The comic was there for his quips; he was *not* supposed to guess the answer. The veterans took care of that, with an arsenal of questions *(below)* refined over the years to elicit a maximum of information with a minimum of effort.

Are you self-employed?

Do you deal in services?

Do you work for a profit-making organization?

Do people come to you? Men and women?

Are they happier when they leave?

Do you need a college education to do what you do?

Do you wear a uniform in doing this?

Is a product involved? Could I hold it in my hand?

Is it bigger than a bread box? Smaller than an elephant?

Ollie the Dragon chats with Kukla before moving in to administer a friendly bite to the nose of the gentle clown.

Affair of the Heart

While parents winced and educators muttered, the nation's first television generation gathered around the flickering blue tube when the sun went down to watch *The Lone Ranger* and *Hopalong Cassidy* beat the outlaws to the draw, to cheer *Lassie* and *Rin-Tin-Tin* as they rescued those in peril, to journey among the stars and the beep-blips of space in the gadget-filled ships of *Space Patrol* and *Captain Midnight*. Millions of small boys donned coonskin caps in emulation of *Disneyland's*

For reasons wholly incomprehensible to me this charming bit of satire . . . and fantasy . . . is . . . about to go off the air. Surely such an assassination, murther and mayhem cannot be permitted in this enlightened land of culture and sophistication. ADLAI STEVENSON

Davy Crockett *(page 59)* and millions of treble voices joined Karen and Doreen in the *Mickey Mouse Club* theme song (M-i-c—k-e-y—M-o-u-s-e). Amidst all the noise one program charmed elders as much as it did children: Burr Tillstrom's gentle puppet show *Kukla, Fran and Ollie*. With no script and virtually no rehearsal, Kukla, the wise and bubbly clown, and sentimental, snaggle-toothed Oliver J. Dragon joined their real-live friend Fran Allison for a chat and a few songs. From time to time other Kuklapolitans were heard from, including Beulah Witch, Madame Ooglepuss, Fletcher Rabbit and Colonel Crackie (Tillstrom used 10 voices in the show, all of them his own). At its height *Kukla, Fran and Ollie* was seen by 10 million viewers on 57 stations and drew some 8,000 letters a week. But the all-important sponsors gradually began to drop away, unwilling to give the prime time of 7:00 p.m. to kids. Squeezed from half an hour down to 15 minutes in 1951, the show finally left the air entirely in 1957. When its demise was announced, NBC was bombarded with letters from devoted *Kukla, Fran and Ollie* fans, one of whom *(above)* was a former Presidential candidate.

The Spectacular

In the '50s, a new phenomenon began to enliven the routine regularly scheduled programming of television. It was the extra-long, one-time-only, painstakingly and expensively produced show called the spectacular, or the special. One of the first extravaganzas appeared on Christmas Eve in 1951: a Nativity opera, *Amahl and the Night Visitors,* written especially for television by composer Gian Carlo Menotti. It was a tremendous success, and by 1959 the networks were advertising close to 400 such specials.

Spectaculars varied in quality as they increased in quantity. NBC's lavish 1954 musical Western, *Satins*

Someone told me when I appeared on a TV spectacular that it would take over 100 years for that many people to hear me in concert. He failed to tell me how many seconds it would take them to forget.

CELLIST GREGOR PIATIGORSKY

---

and Spurs, starring the young veteran Betty Hutton, was such a disaster that after it was over Miss Hutton threatened to quit show business forever. On the other hand, when Mary Martin flew through the air (on wires) as *Peter Pan* on March 7, 1955, one out of every two Americans watched her and, contrary to what another spectacular star suggested *(above),* talked about it for weeks afterward.

But perhaps the most memorable special of the era was a two-hour show aired June 15, 1953, on both CBS and NBC to celebrate the Ford Motor Company's 50th anniversary. The program had a swirling ballet by Jerome Robbins, contralto Marian Anderson singing "The Battle Hymn of the Republic" and Mary Martin doing a delightful spoof on a half-century of women's fashions *(overleaf).* But the show-stopper was a duet by Miss Martin and Ethel Merman, who sat on stools in the middle of a bare stage and sang a medley of 31 songs. For sheer theatrical excitement, nothing yet seen on television had matched their performance; suddenly it was clear that TV could be great entertainment.

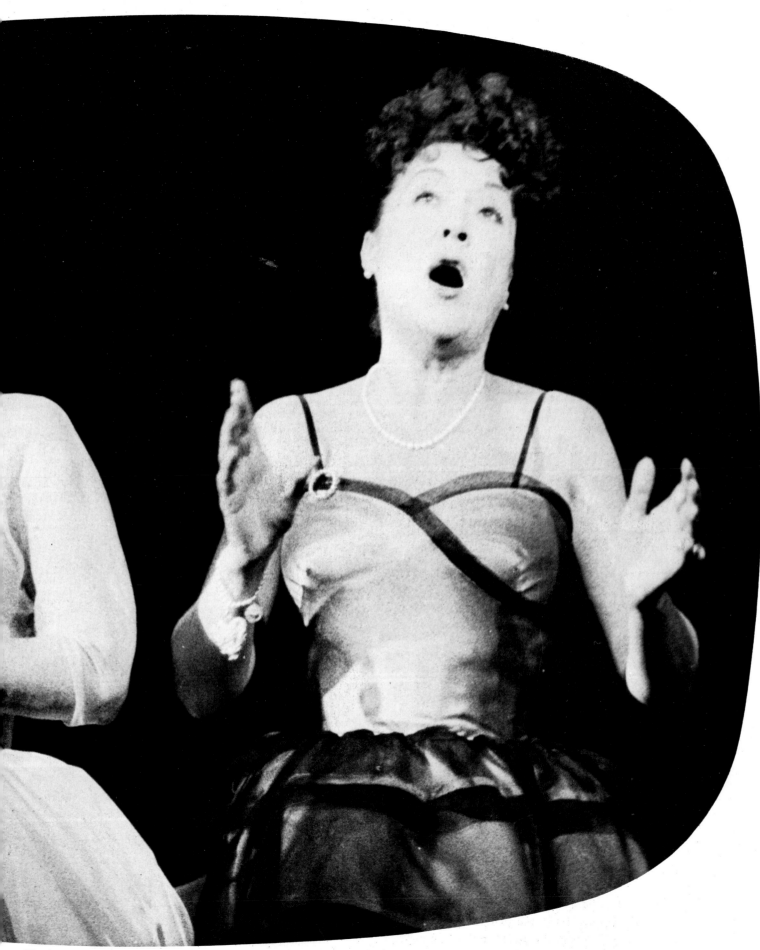

Singing stars Mary Martin and Ethel Merman match styles in their famous duet on the 1953 Ford Anniversary Show.

Mary Martin starts her fashion spoof . . .   *. . . by looking askance at her basic shape.*   *The first change is to 1903's forward*

Now she is the curveless flapper of 1925.   *For 1937, she hunches shoulders and pouts.*   *The 1953 girl seems in sad shape . . . but .*

. with a large feathered hat for balance.

Then she switches to the hobble skirt of 1914

. . . and shows the one-legged look in motion.

zips herself up to face tomorrow unafraid.

Back in basic form at the end of the '50s . . .

Mary marches toward the future . . . and flops!

Though Edward R. Murrow looked relaxed on "See It Now," he smoked up to three packs of cigarettes a day—to steady his nerves.

Style-Setting Commentator

Late in the afternoon of Sunday, November 18, 1951, as millions of Americans looked on in their homes, television began to approach its potential. The premiere of a half hour news show, *See It Now,* simultaneously showed, on a split TV screen, two bridges: New York's Brooklyn and San Francisco's Golden Gate. As cigarette smoke swirled around his lean saturnine face, Edward R. Murrow's flat, dramatic voice said: "For the first time in the history of man we are able to look out at both the Atlantic and Pacific coasts of this great country at the same time . . . no journalistic age was ever given a weapon for truth with quite the scope of this fledgling television."

For the next seven years Murrow used the weapon without letup. *See It Now,* the program he conceived with producer Fred Friendly, ranged over the globe from India to Suez, went to night school in Shreveport, Louisiana, with a 40-year-old Negro who wanted to "learn letters, because letters make words" and to Robert Oppenheimer's laboratory in Princeton, New Jersey. It brought to Americans the hollow sound of an infantryman's shovel scraping a foxhole in a frozen Korean riverbank, and the grim sight of a Buchenwald tattoo on the arm of an Israeli jet pilot.

Some weeks were especially memorable. On October 20, 1953, Murrow said in that apocalyptic voice: "We propose to examine . . . the case of Lieutenant Radulovich." The U.S. Air Force, poisoned by the miasma of McCarthyism, had requested the resignation of the young lieutenant on security grounds, not because *his* loyalty was doubtful but because his father's and sister's were: "We believe that 'the son shall not bear the iniquity of the father,' even though that iniquity be proved; and in this case, it was not." As Murrow finished, technicians and stagehands, strongly moved, shook his hand; five weeks later on the same program the Air Force Secretary was shown restoring Radulovich to duty. *New York Times* TV critic Jack Gould called it "the first time a major network consented to a program taking a vigorous editorial stand . . . a long

step forward." On March 9, 1954, Murrow looked into the camera once more and became the first major commentator to launch a full-dress attack on Senator Joe McCarthy. Across 1,500 miles the same thought occurred next day to editorial writers at both the St. Louis *Post-Dispatch* and the *New York Herald Tribune:* "Television has come of age."

Innovation was nothing new to Ed Murrow. As CBS' European director he had pioneered the live news roundup with broadcasts about the Nazi takeover of Austria; during World War II his nightly broadcasts from embattled Britain (his opening signature was a thunderously quiet: "This—is London") made his the most famous voice in radio. When Murrow shifted to TV—whose news programs featured boutonniered announcers showing still pictures while reading dull press bulletins—it was as if a revolution had been unleashed. An impatient yearning for perfection, an intense social conscience, a sense of mission about informing the people replaced the safe, dull stand-up newscasts. NBC cynics might versify that "Nobody's brow furrows like Edward R. Murrow's" but NBC hastily brought in news commentators with bite and teamed up David Brinkley and Chet Huntley in 1956.

Murrow was changing TV, and TV was proud—and nervous. No one questioned that *See It Now* was a critical success; Murrow and the program together received 20 awards in 1954 alone. But Murrow's social conscience was a bother, getting the company into trouble with politicians, cigarette companies, doctors, rightists. "Why does Murrow have to save the world every week?" growled CBS executives.

In 1955 *See It Now* was shifted from its prime time, which went instead to one of the big-money quiz shows. In 1958 Murrow's old friend and protector William J. Paley, CBS Board Chairman, gave up the fight. "I don't want this constant stomachache," he said. Murrow's retort: "It goes with the job." By the time the decade ended, Murrow had left CBS and TV, bringing down the curtain on one of the industry's proudest, bravest eras.

"Dragnet" Sergeant Joe Friday and Officer Frank Smith question know-it-all landlady Daisy Wilkers about a 476 case—forgery.

Just the Cops, Ma'am

"It was Tuesday, January 11th. It was cool in Los Angeles. We were working the Day Watch out of Forgery Division. My partner's Frank Smith. The boss is Captain Welsh. My name's Friday."

Joe Friday was a TV cop. And for seven years (1952 to 1959) he was *the* cop for the millions of Americans who tuned in *Dragnet* weekly on NBC. Created by Jack Webb—who not only played Friday but directed the show and wrote many of the scripts—*Dragnet* was designed to show crime-busting as it really was. As the program's tagline made clear, its stories essentially were true: "Only the names were changed to protect the innocent." Each episode was based on actual cases taken from the files of the Los Angeles Police Department.

Unlike the shoot-'em-up orgies that had preceded it on radio and TV (*Gangbusters, Your FBI*), *Dragnet* dramatized the routine procedures police used to ferret out criminals. Sergeant Friday and his partner sent suspects' names and descriptions to "R & I" (Records and Identification) and sought their "M O's" (Modus Operandi). The show's set-piece attraction was the low-key questioning by the dour and laconic Sergeant Friday of an endless array of off-beat and equally laconic characters. Throughout the dialogue, Friday would remind them that "all I want is the facts. . . ." In the excerpt below, Friday and Frank Smith seek the facts about a forger who had been using the name of a dead actor to pass bad checks. The witness, Daisy Wilkers, is a devout movie fan who spotted the imposter and immediately called the police.

Audiences loved the show's deadpan realism; during the 1953-1954 season, *Dragnet* was second only to *I Love Lucy* as the most popular show on TV. The program's success bred a half-dozen imitators: CBS launched *Line-Up* in 1954 and ABC followed with *Naked City* in 1958. But none of them matched *Dragnet* in quality or—most importantly—ratings. When the final episode faded from the tube in September 1959, Joe Friday had scored his weekly triumph over the forces of evil, and *Dragnet* was still among the top TV favorites.

THE BIG BOUNCE

DAISY: You the policemen?
JOE: Yes ma'am. *(Shows I.D.)* My name's Friday. . . . This is Frank Smith.
FRANK: Hello.
DAISY: You certainly didn't hurry.
JOE: Traffic was heavy.
DAISY: Why didn't you use your siren?
JOE: Didn't want to scare him off.
DAISY: Too late to worry about that . . . left ten . . . fifteen minutes ago. . . . You might as well come inside.
JOE: Thanks.
DAISY: Suppose you'll want a full report. That's regular procedure, isn't it?
JOE: Go ahead, Miss Wilkers.
DAISY: Well . . . he came up to my door . . . Asked if I had a room for rent. I told him that was what the sign meant. He just laughed . . . like he thought I'd been making a joke. Didn't know I was serious . . . I said I wanted the first month in advance . . . I always insist on a *full month*. . . . Didn't bat an eye. . . . Just brought out his checkbook.
JOE: Now, did he ask if he could make it for a little extra?
DAISY: *(surprised)* How did you know?
JOE: Well, he's been around before.
DAISY: *(sharply)* If he's been around so long, why haven't you picked him up?
JOE: We're trying, ma'am. . . . That's when you called us?
DAISY: Course not. Didn't call you until I was sure the check was no good.
JOE: What made you sure it was phony?

DAISY: The way he signed it.
JOE: *(frowning)* What do you mean?
DAISY: Parker Allington. Trying to make me think he was Parker Allington.
JOE: You knew he wasn't?
DAISY: How could he be? Allington's dead. You didn't know he was dead?
JOE: Yes, ma'am. We knew it. . . . One more thing, Miss Wilkers. . . . We've got a description but it's pretty vague.
DAISY: You mean you want to know who he is?
JOE: Yes ma'am.
DAISY: His name's Wilbur Trench.
JOE: What?
DAISY: Used to play bit parts in pictures. . . . Recognized him the minute he came to the door.

Jerry Lester and Milton Delugg clown as Dagmar waits to read poetry on "Broadway Open House," TV's first late-night talk show.

Steve Allen goes into the audience for some ad-lib conversation.

Cliff Arquette (right) reads a letter from Mama to Jack Paar.

Something for the Night Owls

*Before television 63 per cent of Americans were asleep by
midnight; by 1951 three fourths of those with TV were up late watching the
tube. For the new night owls NBC developed a potpourri of chitchat.
Buxom Dagmar was a stooge for Jerry Lester's slapstick; Steve Allen got the
audience into the act; Jack Paar made tongues wag with his
sometimes risque, always surprising, banter. But the format remained essentially
the same—talk, lots of music and a chance to meet celebrities.*

Live Drama for the Living Room

In 1951 television presented more live dramas (some 400), hired more actors and spent more money ($25 million plus) than all producers and backers of Broadway shows. The reason was not so much that TV was culture-bent as that it faced a quantity of otherwise unfilled air time. Finding material was a problem, and Hollywood, anxiously insisting that "Movies Are Better Than Ever," refused to provide its youthful rival with old films. To make movies expressly for television would have been too costly.

So television was forced to create its own live plays, turning at first to the theater and to novels for stories that could be dramatized. Advertisers eagerly sponsored the programs, and hour-long shows like the Kraft Television Theatre, the U.S. Steel Hour and Philco Playhouse were seen regularly. The proliferation of dramatic shows rapidly reduced the supply of plays and novels; one weekly program was theoretically capable of devouring the entire works of Shakespeare in only a season—and before audiences that would have staggered the Bard. Just as an example, when the Hallmark Hall of Fame presented Hamlet in 1953, probably more people watched it at home than had seen it on the stage in the 350 years since it was written.

The quality of the TV dramatizations varied widely, but some of the fare was excellent. To satisfy the medium's insatiable appetite, ambitious producers and directors like Fred Coe, David Susskind, Arthur Penn

---

MARTY

ANGIE: Boy, you really musta made out good last night.

MARTY: We just talked.

ANGIE: Boy, she must be some talker. She musta been about fifty years old.

CRITIC: I always figger a guy oughtta marry a girl who's twenny years younger than he is, so that when he's forty, his wife is a real nice-looking doll.

TWENTY-YEAR-OLD: That means he'd have to marry the girl when she was one year old.

CRITIC: I never thoughta that.

MARTY: I don't think she was so bad-looking.

ANGIE: She musta kept you inna shadows all night.

CRITIC: Marty, you don't wanna hang around with dogs. It gives you a bad reputation.

ANGIE: Marty, let's go downna bazaar.

MARTY: I told this dog I was gonna call her today.

ANGIE: Brush her.

MARTY: You didn't like her at all?

ANGIE: A nothing. A real nothing.

CRITIC: What's playing on Fordham Road? I think there's a good picture in the Loew's Paradise.

ANGIE: Let's go down to Forty-second Street and walk around. We're sure to wind up with something.

CRITIC: I'll never forgive La Guardia for cutting burlesque outta New York City. . . .

CRITIC: So wadda you figure on doing tonight, Angie?

ANGIE: I don't know. Wadda you figure on doing?

CRITIC: I don't know. *(Turns to the twenty-year-old)* Wadda you figure on doing?

(The twenty-year-old shrugs.

Suddenly Marty brings his fist down on the booth table with a crash. The others turn, startled, toward him. Marty rises in his seat)

MARTY: "What are you doing tonight?" "I don't know, what are you doing?" Burlesque! Loew's Paradise! Miserable and lonely! Miserable and lonely and stupid! What am I, crazy or something?! I got something good! What am I hanging around with you guys for?!

ANGIE: *(A little shocked at Marty's outburst)* Watsa matter with you?

MARTY: *(In a low, intense voice)* You don't like her. My mother don't like her. She's a dog, and I'm a fat, ugly little man. All I know is I had a good time last night. I'm gonna have a good time tonight. If we have enough good times together, I'm going down on my knees and beg that girl to marry me. If we make a party again this New Year's, I gotta date for the party. You don't like her, that's too bad. *(He moves into the booth, sits, turns again to Angie, smiles)* When you gonna get married, Angie? You're thirty-four years old. All your kid brothers are married. You oughtta be ashamed of yourself.

(Still smiling at his private joke, he puts the dime into the slot and then—with a determined finger—he begins to dial)

Marty (Rod Steiger) and his girl, Clara (Nancy Marchand), talk about their loneliness in a scene from Paddy Chayefsky's 1953 play.

THE BACHELOR PARTY by Paddy Chayefsky
THE GOODYEAR TELEVISION PLAYHOUSE

and John Frankenheimer encouraged new authors to turn out fresh scripts. Most of the writers started in obscurity and many ended up the same way. But a few dramatists were launched on brilliant careers, among them Rod Serling *(Requiem for a Heavyweight, Patterns)*, Reginald Rose *(Twelve Angry Men)*, Gore Vidal *(Visit to a Small Planet)* and Paddy Chayefsky *(Marty, The Bachelor Party)*.

Since even the best programs usually were shown only once (video tape did not arrive until 1957), viewers aware of the medium's potential watched regularly. Television drama prospered. But before the decade ended, TV's cultural boom was over—and ironically, Hollywood and film were chiefly responsible for killing it.

Chayefsky's best-known TV effort had been *Marty*, a sensitive story of an awkward and lonely man who turns from his friends *(excerpt on page 274)* to seek comfort in the company of an equally graceless and socially impoverished woman. The play was a tremendous success, and Chayefsky was asked to expand his hourlong script into a full-length film. In 1956 the movie won the Academy Award as the best picture of the year. Soon Hollywood was seeking other TV dramas—and then began wooing the playwrights themselves. The lure of Hollywood was almost irresistible—especially after Chayefsky disclosed that he had made more from his movie adaptation of *Marty* than for all the scripts he wrote for television in a year. Tad Mosel, J. P. Miller, David Shaw and other leading TV playwrights also began to look to film and Broadway.

Actors followed suit. A number who had got their start on television—Rod Steiger, James Dean, Grace Kelly, Paul Newman, Anne Bancroft, Joanne Woodward, Eva Marie Saint—also found that the movies provided not only greater financial rewards, but more fame and a more leisurely working pace.

The final knell of live TV drama was sounded when the movie and TV industries settled their feud. Soon, both began to produce films for television, and the rationale for original, live television drama disappeared.

CHILD OF OUR TIME by Michel del Castillo
PLAYHOUSE 90 (adapted)

REQUIEM FOR A HEAVYWEIGHT by Rod Serling
PLAYHOUSE 90

LITTLE MOON OF ALBAN by James Costigan
HALLMARK HALL OF FAME

THE GREAT ESCAPE by Paul Brickhall
PHILCO TELEVISION PLAYHOUSE (adapted)

TWELVE ANGRY MEN by Reginald Rose
STUDIO ONE

1984 by George Orwell
STUDIO ONE (adapted)

THE DAYS OF WINE AND ROSES by J. P. Miller
PLAYHOUSE 90

PATTERNS by Rod Serling
KRAFT TELEVISION THEATRE

A Week's Delights on the Tube

Saturday

3-4:30 — BROADWAY TV THEATRE: "George and Margaret," With Ernest Truex, Sylvia Field — (9).

3:45-4 — WHAT'S YOUR TROUBLE? — "The Successful Marriage," The Rev. and Mrs. Norman Vincent Peale — (2).

4-4:30 — MR. WIZARD, Science, With Don Herbert — (4).

4:30-5 — BETWEEN THE LINES: "Are Congressional Investigations Helping Morale of Teachers in New York?" — Robert Morris, Dr. Corliss Lamont, George A. Timone, Prof. H. H. Wilson, Guests — (4).

5-5:30 — IT'S A PROBLEM: "New Baby in the Home" — Dr. Helen Wallace, Dr. Emil Piana, Mrs. Clara S. Littledale — (4).

5:30-6 — THROUGH THE ENCHANTED GATE: "Easter Parade," With Victor D'Amico — (4).

6:30-7 — WHAT IN THE WORLD: Dr. Sherman Lee, Curator of Oriental Art at Cleveland Museum, Guest — (2).

7-7:30 — PAUL WHITEMAN TEEN CLUB: With Nancy Lewis — (7).

7:30-8 — BEAT THE CLOCK: With Bud Collyer — (2).

7:30-8 — JOHNNY JUPITER: Satirical Fantasy, on American Life, as Seen by Inhabitants of Planet Jupiter — (5).

7:30-8 — WHAT'S THE BID: Auction-Liberal Bill — (7).

8-9 — JACKIE GLEASON SHOW: Jan Peerce, Guest — (2).

8-9 — ALL-STAR REVUE: With George Jessel, Eddie Cantor, Fred Allen, Gloria De Haven, Guests — (4).

8:30-9 — INTERNATIONAL MOTOR SPORTS SHOW: From Grand Central Palace — (11).

Hit Parade Singers

9-9:30 — THIS IS SHOW BUSINESS: Clifton Fadiman, Host; Jacqueline Susann, Nat Cole, Nora Kaye, Guests — (2).

9-10:30 — SHOW OF SHOWS: With Sid Caesar, Imogene Coca, Marguerite Piazza, Hostess — (4).

9 — LIGHTWEIGHT BOUT: Johnny Gonsalves vs. Virgil Akins, from Chicago's Rainbow Arena — (7).

10:30-11 — IT'S NEWS TO ME: Panel Quiz, John Daly — (2).

10:30-11 — YOUR HIT PARADE: With Snooky Lanson, Dorothy Collins, June Valli — (4).

10:30-11 — AMERICA SPEAKS: "Korean Truce — What It Means to Our Economy" — Ben Limb, Ambassador at Large to the U. N., Guest; Don Passante, Moderator — (9) (Première).

Sunday

11:30 A. M.-1:30 — EASTER PARADE, From Park Ave. — (11); 12:30-1:30 — Fifth Ave. — (4); 1-2 — (2, 7).

3-3:30 — VICTORY AT SEA — (4).

3:30-4 — YOUTH WANTS TO KNOW: Senator Wayne Morse, Guest — (4).

Sullivan and Dancers

4-4:30 — STATE OF THE NATION: Martin P. Durkin, Secretary of Labor — (2).

4:30-6 — OMNIBUS: "Everyman," Burgess Meredith; Grandma Moses at Home; "Trip to the Moon"; Other Features; Alistair Cooke, Narrator — (2).

5-5:30 — HALL OF FAME THEATRE: "The Other Wise Man," Wesley Addy — (4).

5:30-5:45 — SIGHTSEEING WITH SWAYZE — (4) (Première).

6-6:30 — YOU ARE THERE: "The Conquest of Mexico" — (2).

6-6:30 — MEET THE PRESS: Douglas McKay, Secretary of Interior — (4).

6-7 — NEW YORK TIMES YOUTH FORUM: "What Does Religion Mean to Youth?" Dorothy Gordon, Moderator — (5).

6:30-7 — SEE IT NOW, With Edward R. Murrow, Narrator — (2).

7:30-8 — MR. PEEPERS: Wally Cox — (4).

7:30-8:30 — OPERA CAMEOS: "Cavalleria Rusticana," With Rina Telli, Soprano; Martha Lipton, Mezzo-Soprano; Jon Grain, Tenor; Richard Torigi, Baritone — (11).

8-9 — TOAST OF THE TOWN: Ed Sullivan; Notre Dame Glee Club; Gracie Fields, Cab Calloway, Others, Guests — (2).

8-9 — COMEDY HOUR: Donald O'Connor, Brian Aherne, Vivian Blaine — (4).

9-9:30 — FRED WARING SHOW — (2).

9-10 — TELEVISION PLAYHOUSE: "Young Lady of Property," Kim Stanley — (4).

9:30-10 — KEN MURRAY SHOW — (2).

10-10:30 — WEB: "Cry of Trumpets" — (2).

10-10:30 — ARTHUR MURRAY SHOW: With Charles Coburn, Lisa Kirk, Christine Jorgensen, Guests — (5).

10:30-11 — WHAT'S MY LINE — (2).

10:30-11 — FAVORITE STORY — (4).

Monday

7:30-8 — HOLLYWOOD SCREEN TEST: Mary Sinclair — (7).

7:30-8:55 — BROADWAY TV THEATRE: "Wuthering Heights," With William Prince and Meg Mundy — (9).

8-8:30 — GEORGE BURNS AND GRACIE ALLEN — (2).

8-8:30 — PAUL WINCHELL-JERRY MAHONEY — (4).

8:30-9 — ARTHUR GODFREY TALENT SCOUTS — (2).

8:30-9 — JEROME HINES, Basso; Barlow Orchestra — (4).

8:30-9 — JOHNS HOPKINS SCIENCE REVIEW: Sir Roger Makins, Guest — (5).

8:30-9:30 — METROPOLITAN OPERA JAMBOREE: Symphony Orchestra; Soloists; Deems Taylor, Howard Dietz; Others — (7).

9-9:30 — "I LOVE LUCY"; Lucille Ball and Desi Arnaz — (2).

9-9:30 — EYEWITNESS — MYSTERY: "Apartment 4-D," With Nita Talbot; Lee Bowman, Host — (4).

9-9:30 — NEWS-O-RAMA: Columbia University Forum — (11).

9:30-10 — RED BUTTONS SHOW: Gisele MacKenzie, Guest — (2).

9:30-10:30 — ROBERT MONTGOMERY PRESENTS: "Second-Hand Sofa," With Ann Rutherford, Leslie Nielsen — (4).

10-11 — STUDIO ONE: "Shadow of the Devil," With Mercedes McCambridge and James Dunn — (2).

11-11:15 — CHRONOSCOPE: Senator Wayne Morse — (2).

Tuesday

11 A. M. — SENATE INTERNAL SECURITY SUBCOMMITTEE, Investigating Communism in American Education, Senator William Jenner, Chairman; Herbert Philbrick, Witness — (4).

7:30-7:45 — THE DINAH SHORE SHOW — (4).

7:45-8 — JANE FROMAN'S U.S.A. CANTEEN — (2).

8-9 — ERNIE KOVACS SHOW: With Dorothy Richards, Eddie Hatrak, Trigger Lund and Andy McKay — (2).

8-9 — STAR THEATRE: With Milton Berle, Cesar Romero, Laraine Day, Kathryn Murray, Guests — (4).

8:30 – BISHOP FULTON J. SHEEN – (5).

30-9 – THE BIG ISSUE: "Should Communists Be Permitted to Teach in Colleges?" – Corliss Lamont, James Burnham – (5).

9:30 – CITY HOSPITAL: With Melville Ruick – (2).

9:30 – FIRESIDE THEATRE: "Cocoon," Barbara Brown – (4).

– FEATHERWEIGHT BOUT: Bill Bossio vs. Miquel Berrios, from Ridgewood Grove, Brooklyn – (7).

– PRO-BASKETBALL PLAYOFFS: Knickerbockers vs. Minneapolis Lakers, from 69th Regiment Armory – (11).

30-10 – AUTOMOBILE SHOW, from the Waldorf-Astoria Hotel, With Irene Dunne, Hostess – (2).

30-10 – CIRCLE THEATRE: "A Slight Case of April," With Hildy Parks and Others – (4).

-10:30 – DANGER: "Family Jewels," With Gary Merrill – (2).

-10:30 – TWO FOR THE MONEY, Quiz, Herb Shriner – (4).

:30-11 – SHOWCASE: "Monkey's Paw," Una Merkel – (2).

-11:30 – AN EVENING WITH HARRY HERSHFIELD – (7).

Kovacs' Clowns

Wednesday

A. M. – SENATE ARMED SERVICES SUBCOMMITTEE, Hearings on Alleged Ammo Shortages in Korea. With Former Secretary of Defense, Robert Lovett, and Assistant Secretary of Defense W. J. McNeil, Witnesses – (4).

7:25 – GOVERNOR DEWEY: "New York City's Finances." With Lieut. Gov. Moore, State Comptroller J. Raymond McGovern. Others – (2).

7:30 – MARCH OF TIME: "Omaha, Rail Metropolis on the Plains" – (4).

15-7:30 – THIS IS CHARLES LAUGHTON: Readings – (11).

30-8 – DATE WITH JUDY: With Mary Linn Beller – (7).

30-8:55 – BROADWAY TV THEATRE: "Wuthering Heights," With William Prince, Meg Mundy – (9).

45-8 – THE PERRY COMO SHOW – (2).

8-9 – ARTHUR GODFREY AND HIS FRIENDS: With Frank Parker, Marion Marlowe, Janette Davis – (2).

8-8:30 – I MARRIED JOAN: With Joan Davis – (4).

8-9 – JUNIOR TOWN MEETING: "Freedom for Enslaved Peoples" – High School Students, Guests – (13).

8:30-9 – MUSIC HALL: Patti Page, Ezio Pinza, Guest – (4).

9-10 – TELEVISION THEATRE: "Next of Kin," With Frederic Tozere, James Daly, Jack Arthur, Pat Ferris – (4).

9-10 – STAGE A NUMBER, Talent Variety Show – (5).

9 – PRO-BASKETBALL PLAYOFFS: Knickerbockers vs. Minneapolis Lakers, from 69th Regiment Armory – (11).

9:30-10 – MAN AGAINST CRIME: With Ralph Bellamy – (2).

10 – FEATHERWEIGHT BOUT: Percy Bassett vs. Davey Gallardo, from Washington – (2).

Godfrey and Tony Marvin

Thursday

11 A. M. – SENATE ARMED SERVICES SUBCOMMITTEE, Hearings on Alleged Ammo Shortages in Korea. With Former Defense Secretary, Robert Lovett, Witness; Senator Margaret Chase Smith, Chairman – (4).

7-7:15 – SAMMY KAYE SHOW: With Jean Martin – (4).

7:30-7:45 – DINAH SHORE SHOW – (4).

7:45-8 – JANE FROMAN'S U.S.A. CANTEEN – (2).

8-8:30 – LIFE WITH LUIGI: Vito Scotti – (2) (Première).

8-8:30 – GROUCHO MARX: "You Bet Your Life" – (4).

8:30-9 – FOUR-STAR PLAYHOUSE: "Dante's Inferno," With Dick Powell, Regis Toomey – (2).

8:30-9 – TREASURY MEN IN ACTION: With Walter Greaza – (4).

8:30-9 – CHANCE OF A LIFETIME: Georgie Price, Guest – (7).

9-9:30 – VIDEO THEATRE: "With Glory and Honor," With Wendell Corey and Others – (2).

9-9:30 – DRAGNET, With Jack Webb – (4).

9 – LIGHT HEAVYWEIGHT BOUT: Chuck Speiser vs. Billy Fifield, from Detroit – (7).

9:30-10 – BIG TOWN: With Patrick McVey, Jane Nigh – (2).

9:30-10 – PLAY: "Just What the Doctor Ordered," With Joanne Dru, Scott Brady, Lisa Ferraday – (4).

9:30-10 – WHAT'S THE STORY: Panel News Quiz – (5).

10-10:30 – MY LITTLE MARGIE: With Gale Storm – (2).

10-10:30 – AUTHOR MEETS THE CRITICS: "Democratic Socialism." Norman Thomas, Prof. Leo Wollman, Michael Straight, Virgillia Peterson, Moderator – (5).

10:30-11 – FOREIGN INTRIGUE: With Jerome Thor – (4).

Groucho and Fenniman

Friday

8-8:30 – MAMA, With Peggy Wood – (2).

8-8:30 – DENNIS DAY SHOW: From Hollywood – (4).

8-8:30 – ADVENTURES OF OZZIE AND HARRIET – (7).

8:30-9 – MY FRIEND IRMA, Marie Wilson, Cathy Lewis – (2).

8:30-9 – THE LIFE OF RILEY, With William Bendix, Marjorie Reynolds and Others – (4).

8:45-9 – RUDOLPH HALLEY REPORTS – (7).

9-9:30 – PLAYHOUSE OF STARS: "The Mirror," With Victor Jory, Ian MacDonald – (2).

9-9:30 – THE BIG STORY: A Reporter's Assignment – (4).

9-9:30 – LIFE BEGINS AT EIGHTY – (5, 13).

9 – PRO-BASKETBALL PLAYOFFS: Knickerbockers vs. Minneapolis Lakers, from the 69th Regiment Armory – (11).

9:30-10 – OUR MISS BROOKS, With Eve Arden – (2).

9:30-10 – THE ALDRICH FAMILY, With Bobby Ellis – (4).

9:30-10 – TALES OF TOMORROW: "Homecoming," With Edith Fellows and Others – (7).

10-10:30 – MR. AND MRS. NORTH: With Richard Denning, Barbara Britton – (2).

10 – MIDDLEWEIGHT BOUT: Jimmy Beau vs. Randy Sandy, from the St. Nicholas Arena – (4).

10-10:30 – TWENTY QUESTIONS: Blanche Thebom, Guest – (5).

"Ding Dong School's" Miss Frances clangs the school bell.

Loretta Young ends by reading aloud some homely wisdom.

Betty Furness says goodnight for her new refrigerator.

A spotlighted Durante says "Goodnight, Mrs. Calabash."

Red Buttons soft-shoes it offstage to his "Ho-Ho Song."

"Peace," says Dave Garroway, signing off for "Today."

Having advised her listeners to "See the U.S.A. in your Chevrolet," Dinah Shore ends her show by blowing a big, smacking kiss.

Picture Credits

Fabric design by Charles Mikolaycak.

6,7—Yale Joel. 8,9—Cornell Capa from Magnum. 10,11—J.R. Eyerman. 12,13—Alfred Eisenstaedt. 14,15—Yale Joel. 16,17—Carl Iwasaki. 18 through 21—Grey Villet. 22,23—Dmitri Kessel. 24—"Think Maybe We'd Better Say Something About It?" from Herblock's Here And Now (Simon & Schuster, 1955). 28—Fred O. Seibel for The Richmond Times-Dispatch; Fitzpatrick for St. Louis Post-Dispatch—"I'm Fine. Of Course, Every Once In A While I Go Like This": from Herblock's Special for Today (Simon & Schuster, 1958); Frank Williams. 29—"What's Our Firm, Unswerving Asian Policy This Week?" from Herblock's Here and Now (Simon & Schuster, 1955). 85—Harold M. Talburt courtesy Scripps-Howard Newspapers—Bill Mauldin © 1960 St. Louis Post-Dispatch; Hugh Haynie for The Louisville Courier Journal. 32,33—Milton H. Greene. 35—Al Freni. 36,37—Pictorial Parade. 39—Carl Mydans. 40,41—Hy Peskin. 42—Hank Walker. 45—NBC. 46—Karen Radkai photograph for Vogue: Copyright © 1958 by the Condé Nast Publications Inc.; Courtesy of Monsanto Company—Courtesy The McCall Publishing Company; Courtesy Johnson & Johnson; Courtesy Monet Jewelers. 47—Courtesy Luis Estévez; Photographed by Richard Avedon courtesy Fairfax, Inc.; Photographed by Milton H. Greene courtesy LIFE magazine—No Credit; Photographed by Richard Avedon courtesy Harper's Bazaar. 48,49—Alfred Eisenstaedt. 51—Cornell Capa. 53—Don Uhrbrock. 54,55—Richard Avedon. 56,57—J.R. Eyerman. 59—John Dominis. 60—Joe Munroe; Ralph Crane. 61—Bill Bridges. 62,63—Brown Brothers; Ralph Morse. 64—© Philippe Halsman. 65—Copyright © by Roger Price—© Philippe Halsman. 68,69—Carl Iwasaki except top United Press International. 70—Orin Sealy for Denver Post. 71—Carl Iwasaki (2)—Courtesy Doubleday & Co., Inc.; Bert Brandt. 72,73—Loomis Dean—Andreas Feininger; © 1951, New York Herald Tribune Inc. Reprinted with permission of W.C.C. Publishing Company, Inc. 74,75—Joe Clark; John Raymond Solowinski; Floyd Bowser; Paul Schutzer; Gordon Tenney from Black Star; Yale Joel. 76,77—Left Herb Alden. Center Nina Leen. Right Carl Iwasaki. 78,79—Lisa Larsen; Gordon Parks; Nina Leen (3). 82,83—Fred W. McDarrah from The Beat Scene (Corinth Books, 1959). 85—Burt Glinn from Magnum. 86,87—Harry Redl for TIME, Joern Gerdts. 90—N.R. Farbman. 91—Fred DeWitt for TIME. 92—Charles Bonnay for Paris-Match. 93—Burt Glinn from Magnum. 94,95—Gray Villet. 97—Michael Rougier. 98 through 101—Alfred Eisenstaedt. 102—Lisa Larsen. 103—Alfred Eisenstaedt. 104—Alfred Eisenstaedt except right United Press International. 105—Alfred Eisenstaedt (2)—Lisa Larsen. 106,107—Lisa Larsen. 108,109—Burt Glinn from Magnum. 110—Hy Peskin; George Silk—Alfred Eisenstaedt. 111—Edward Clark; Ralph Morse—Hy Peskin; George Skadding (2). 112—George Skadding—Hank Walker; Ralph Morse—Hank Walker. 113—Hank Walker—Hank Walker; Hy Peskin—George Skadding. Backgrounds 110 through 113—Ralph Morse. 114,115—George Skadding except buttons Sy Seidman. 120,121—Hank Walker. 122,123—Hank Walker; Yale Joel. 125—Hank Walker. 126,127—Leonard McCombe. 128,129—Robert Phillips from Black Star. 130,131—Hank Walker. 133—"I Can't Do This To Me"—from Herblock's Here And Now (Simon & Schuster, 1955). 134,135—Paul Schutzer. 137—Slim Aarons. 138—Milton H. Greene; United Press International; Brown Brothers. 139—Photo Files. 140,141—All courtesy Alice Baker, Culver Pictures, Terry Drucker, Helen Greenway, Carol Isenberg, Merit Music Shop, Inc., Jean Morein, Photo Files, and Mary Steinbauer. 142,143—Cliff Segerblom (3). 144,145—Don Wright. 146—Paul Schutzer except center Alfred Eisenstaedt. 147—Allan Grant; Leviton-Atlanta—Paul Schutzer; Ralph Crane. 148 through 151—Paul Schutzer. 153—Ralph Morse. 154,155—Joe Scherschel. 157—Dick Ericson. 158—Drawing by Claude; Copr. © 1956 The New Yorker Magazine, Inc.—David Lees. 159—Dan Weiner for FORTUNE. 160,161—Pete Wyma; Bob Sherman

—Ron Partridge. 162,163—Ralph Crane; Henry Boltinoff. 164—Kaufman for McCall's—Bern Keating from Black Star. 165—Yale Joel. 166, 167—© Saturday Evening Post, 1954—Joe Scherschel; Ralph Crane. 168,169—Stan Fine; Sol Libsohn for FORTUNE. 170—Erich Hartmann from Magnum. 171—Irwin Caplan—Joe Clark. 172,173—Harry Jones, Star Weekly; Ralph Crane. 174,175—Dennis Stock from Magnum. 177—Bill Ray. 178,179—Rudolph Burkhardt. 180—Ladies' Home Journal. 181—Courtesy of The Coca-Cola Company, copyright owner and owner of the registered trademarks "Coca-Cola" and "Coke." 182,183—John Zimmerman—Craft Master Corporation. 184—Courtesy Herman Levin. 185—Leonard McCombe. 186,187—Eliot Elisofon; Courtesy Kermit Bloomgarden. 188—Courtesy Edward Padula; Jerry Cooke—Courtesy Harold Prince. 189—Hank Walker. 190,191—Courtesy Carmen Capalbo; Richard Avedon. 192—E.P. Dutton and Co., Inc. 193—Peter Stackpole. 194—Doubleday & Co., Inc.; Little, Brown & Co. 195—Simon and Schuster, Inc.; Charles Scribner's Sons. 196—Prentice-Hall, Inc.; Courtesy A.C. Spectorsky—McGraw-Hill—David McKay Co., Inc.; Doubleday & Co., Inc.; Rand McNally & Co. 197—Prentice-Hall, Inc.; Oxford University Press—Prentice Hall, Inc.; The Dial Press, Inc. 198,199—Sy Seidman. 200—Copyright 1949 by Cowles Communications, Inc.; Copyright © 1953 by HMH Publishing Co. Inc.—SPORTS ILLUSTRATED—Copyright © 1952 by E.C. Publications, Inc.; Copyright 1951 by Johnson Publishing Co., Inc., Chicago, Illinois; Reprinted from TV Guide ® with permission. Copyright © 1953 by Triangle Publications Inc. 201—Courtesy David Maness. 205—Garrett-Howard courtesy Modern Screen, Dell Publishing Co., Inc. 206,207—Milton H. Greene; Culver Pictures; United Press International—Springer-Bettmann Film Archive; Allan Grant. 208,209—Thomas McAvoy. 210—Los Angeles Examiner from United Press International. 211—Wide World; Los Angeles Times. 212—Wide World; Globe Photos—Springer-Bettmann Film Archive—Culver Pictures. 213—Peter Stackpole; Nat Dallinger from Gilloon Agency—Wide World; Ralph Crane. 214—Modern Screen, Dell Publishing Co., Inc. 215—Culver Pictures. 216—Left United Press International—Nat Dallinger from Gilloon Agency. Center United Press International. Right Wide World—Springer-Bettmann Film Archive—United Press International. 217—United Press International; Frank Horch—United Press International—Wide World. 218—Globe Photos. 219—Leonard McCombe. 220—All courtesy Culver Pictures, Modern Screen, Dell Publishing Co., Inc., Photo Files, United Press International and Wide World. 223—Brown Brothers. 224—All Culver Pictures except top right G.B.D. International Films and bottom left No Credit. 225—All Culver Pictures except bottom left Alfred Eisenstaedt. 226,227—From SICK, SICK, SICK by Jules Feiffer. Copyright © 1956, 1957, 1958 by Jules Feiffer. Used with permission of McGraw-Hill Book Company. 228—Sy Friedman. 229—Peter Stackpole. 230,231—Mark Shaw. 232,233—Ken Heyman. 235—Joseph Sterling. 236,237—Bruce Davidson from Magnum. 238,239—Bruce Davidson from Magnum; Leonard McCombe. 240,241—Bruce Davidson from Magnum. 242—Joseph Sterling. 243—Bruce Davidson from Magnum. 244,245—George Haling. 248,249—Allan Grant. 251—Wide World. 252—Loomis Dean. 253—No Credit—Loomis Dean—Culver Pictures. 254—Martha Holmes; No Credit—ABC Television Network; Culver Pictures—CBS; Robert Willoughby. 255—No Credit; Culver Pictures—Culver Pictures; No Credit—ABC Television Network; Culver Pictures. 256—Art Selby. 257,258—NBC. 260 through 263—Culver Pictures. 264,265—Wide World. 266,267—Slim Aarons. 268—CBS. 270—Courtesy Jack Webb, NBC. 272—Culver Pictures. 273—Culver Pictures; Cornell Capa from Magnum. 275—Culver Pictures. 276—Culver Pictures—Bill Bridges—CBS. 277—NBC; Brown Brothers—No Credit; Allan Grant—CBS; Brown Brothers. 278—Brown Brothers; Frederic Lewis. 279—Ralph Morse; CBS; No Credit. 280—NBC; Courtesy Loretta Young—Culver Pictures (4). 281—Wide World.

Acknowledgments

The editors of this book wish to thank the following persons and institutions for their assistance:

Mrs. Eve Bayne, Chief Librarian, Dell Publishing Co. Inc., New York City; Ruth P. Braun, Chief Librarian, *The Detroit News;* Bill Bridges, Los Angeles; Sid Caesar, Los Angeles; Fred Coe, New York City; Frank Driggs, New York City; Gabe Essoe, Publicist, Walt Disney Productions, Burbank, California; Mark Greenberg, MacFadden-Bartell Corp., New York City; Garth Hamby, The Coca-Cola Company, Atlanta, Georgia; Stephen Holden, New York City; Roy L. King, Chief Librarian, St. *Louis Post-Dispatch;* Lawrence Lariar, Freeport, New York; Mitchell Lewis, McLendon Corp., Dallas; Jack Meltzer, New York City; Joseph Molloy, *Philadelphia Inquirer;* Joseph Nettis, Philadelphia; Mrs. Pat Pappas, *Playboy* magazine, Chicago; Mildred Simpson, Librarian, Academy of Motion Picture Arts and Sciences, Los Angeles; Tony Spina, Chief Photographer, *Detroit Free Press;* Ty Triplett, The Five-State Edsel Club, Grosse Pointe, Michigan; Leigh Weiner, Los Angeles.

Bibliography

Anderson, Jack and Ronald W. May, *McCarthy: The Man, The Senator, The "Ism."* The Beacon Press, 1952.

Bellaire, Arthur, *TV Advertising.* Harper & Bros., 1959.

Block, Haskell M. and Robert G. Sheed, *Masters of Modern Drama.* Random House, Inc., 1962.

Blum, Daniel, *Pictorial History of Television.* Chilton Co., 1959.

Bogart, Leo, *The Age of Television.* Frederick Ungar Publishing Co., 1956.

Friendly, Fred W., *Due to Circumstances Beyond Our Control....* Random House, Inc., 1967.

Friendly, Fred W. and Edward R. Murrow, eds., *See It Now.* Simon & Schuster, Inc., 1955.

Goldman, Eric F., *The Crucial Decade—And After.* Random House, Inc., 1960.

Guiles, F. L., *Norma Jean.* McGraw-Hill, Inc., 1969.

Kendrick, Alexander, *Prime Time.* Little, Brown and Co., 1967.

King, Martin Luther, Jr., *Stride Toward Freedom.* Ballantine Books, Inc., 1958.

Moss, Norman, *Men Who Play God.* Harper & Row, 1968.

Rovere, Richard H., *Senator Joe McCarthy.* Harcourt, Brace and Co., 1959.

Sann, Paul, *Fads, Follies and Delusions of the American People.* Crown Publishers, Inc., 1967.

Serling, Rod, *Patterns.* Simon & Schuster, Inc., 1957.

Settel, Irving and William Laas, *A Pictorial History of Television.* Grosset & Dunlap, Inc., 1969.

Shepley, James R., and Clay Blair Jr., *The Hydrogen Bomb.* David McKay Company, Inc., 1954.

Shulman, Arthur and Roger Youman, *How Sweet It Was.* Bonanza Books, 1966.

Whitman, Alden R. and The New York Times, *Portrait: Adlai E. Stevenson.* Harper & Row, 1965.

Text Credits

37—From *Midcentury* by John Dos Passos, Houghton Mifflin Co., 1960, pp. 479-480. 50—Quotes from *Adlai Stevenson, A Study in Values* by Herbert J. Muller, Copyright © 1967 by Herbert J. Muller, p. 230; *Portrait: Adlai E. Stevenson* by Alden Whitman and *The New York Times,* Harper & Row, 1965, p. 181; *Adlai Stevenson's Public Years* by Adlai Stevenson, Copyright 1966 by Grossman, pp. 31, 58. 81—"Here's Prunes in Your Teeth" by John Crosby, courtesy *New York Herald Tribune;* Excerpt from "A Square Is A Square Is A?" by Herbert Mitgang, © 1959 by The New York Times Company. Reprinted by permission. 88-89 —From "The Origin of the Beat Generation" by Jack Kerouac: originally appeared in *Playboy* magazine, © 1959 by Jack Kerouac. Reprinted by permission of Sterling Lord Agency; From *On the Road* by Jack Kerouac, © 1955, 1957 by Jack Kerouac. Reprinted by permission of The Viking Press, Inc.; From *"Howl" and Other Poems* by Allen Ginsberg, © 1956, 1959 by Allen Ginsberg. Reprinted by permission of City Lights Books: From *The Happy Birthday of Death* by Gregory Corso, © 1960 by New Directions Publishing Corporation. Reprinted by permission of the copyright holder. 152—*Cash Box* magazine. 192—From *Kiss Me, Deadly* by Mickey Spillane, Copyright 1952 by E.P. Dutton & Co., Inc. Reprinted by permission, pp. 247-248. 194—From *The Caine Mutiny* by Herman Wouk, Copyright 1951, by Herman Wouk. Reprinted by permission of Doubleday & Company, Inc., pp. 150-151. 194-195—From *The Catcher in the Rye* by J. D. Salinger, Copyright 1945, 1946, 1951, by J. D. Salinger. Courtesy Little, Brown and Company, pp. 224-225. 195—From *Peyton Place,* © Copyright 1956 by Grace Metalious. Reprinted by permission of Simon & Schuster, Inc., pp. 277-278; From *From Here to Eternity* by James Jones, Copyright 1951, by James Jones. Courtesy Charles Scribner's Sons, p. 219. 205-221—Miscellaneous quotes throughout from *Photoplay* used with permission of Macfadden-Bartell Corp. 208-209—Courtesy *Modern Screen,* April and May 1956, Dell Publishing Co. Inc. 210-211—Courtesy *Modern Screen,* March 1958, Dell Publishing Co. Inc.; Courtesy *Movie Mirror,* December 1958 and November 1959, © 1958 and 1959, Sterling Group Inc. 218—Courtesy *Modern Screen,* March 1959, Dell Publishing Co. Inc. 226—William K. Zinsser, "American Humor, 1966" Horizon © 1966 American Heritage Publishing Co., Inc. 228-229—Courtesy Shelley Berman and Mort Sahl. 230—© 1961, 1970 by Mike Nichols and Elaine May. 246-247—Excerpts abridged from *The Shook-Up Generation* by Harrison E. Salisbury, © 1958 Harrison E. Salisbury. Reproduced by permission of Harper & Row, pp. 18-21, 30, 41-42. 258-259—Script courtesy of Mel Brooks, Mel Tokin and Tony Webster. 272—*Dragnet* script courtesy Jack Webb and NBC. 278-279—© 1953 by The New York Times Company. Reprinted by permission.

Index

Printed in U.S.A.

XXXX